WRITE ON THE WALL

A how-to guide for effective planning in groups

By B. Terence Goodwin

 **ASTD**

AMERICAN SOCIETY
FOR TRAINING AND
DEVELOPMENT

1640 KING STREET
BOX 1443
ALEXANDRIA,VIRGINIA
22313-2043

703/683-8100
FAX 703/683-8103

WRITE ON THE WALL

Ordering information: Books published by the American Society for Training and Development can be ordered by calling 703/683-8100.

Library of Congress Catalog Card Number: 93-74579

ISBN: 1-56286-001-1

.

ASTD

AMERICAN SOCIETY
FOR TRAINING AND
DEVELOPMENT

1640 KING STREET
BOX 1443
ALEXANDRIA, VIRGINIA
22313-2043

703/683-8100
FAX 703/683-8103

CONTENTS

INTRODUCTION

Despite many businesses' zealous interest in strategic planning and their increased emphasis on project planning and management, there is a planning vacuum in much of the United States that is stifling the country's competitiveness and performance. In fact, many businesses and nonprofit organizations do no real planning whatsoever. At best, many prepare annual budgets and then have periodic meetings to decide how they are going to deal with this week's problem or opportunity. This type of haphazard operational approach wastes time, money, and energy and is simply not good for business.

Of course there is a solution to the problem: Increase the amount of planning that takes place, and improve the methods for developing plans. The fact that you are reading this book indicates your interest in planning. And this book will show you how to lead a team through a group planning process.

A Leader's Role
Group endeavors don't succeed without leadership. Today's leader is one who directs a participatory process—a process in which members of a group are motivated to share the responsibility for planning and managing a project.

What To Expect From This Book
This book explains how to lead a team through a group planning process. Section 1 addresses the key aspects to preplanning. Chapter 1 explores the benefits of conducting brainstorming sessions and describes what a group leader should determine when group planning is being considered. Chapters 2 and 3 examine the role of the meeting

facilitator and describe in detail what the facilitator must do to help the group create a written, action-oriented plan.

Chapter 4 presents the tools needed to conduct productive meetings, and chapter 5 shows why its important to conduct a preplanning project meeting to get ready for group participation. Practical advice on how to achieve and maintain focus is provided. In fact, the *Write on the Wall* process itself is a major element of focused group planning.

Section 2 describes in detail what you and the group must do from the first meeting to the last. Whether your group needs a business plan, marketing plan, advertising plan, or public relations plan, this book explains how you can do it in a group setting. Chapters 6 through 9 describe how to build a strategic business plan based on the formats outlined in chapter 5. Chapter 10 explains how to develop an action plan that gets results.

Section 3 addresses the importance of visioning, documenting financial justification for a plan, and training facilitators to lead group planning projects. Chapter 11 describes how important it is for a plan to complement an organization's long-term outlook and provides a step-by-step guide for conducting a visioning exercise. It also explains the importance of thoroughly documenting the financial feasibility of any plan. Chapter 12 explains how a trainer can positively affect the group planning process and provides a training workshop format that can be used to teach group planning and facilitation skills.

Finally, section 4 illustrates a few plan variations that can be used to address specific situations. Specifically, Chapter 13 describes how to develop an advertising plan, and chapter 14 describes the components of public relations planning.

The *Write on the Wall* planning process focuses on people and how their creativity can be intensified in a group setting. The process produces straightforward plans that usually consist of a few sheets of paper that are used frequently to guide a group through its project implementation. They are repeatedly referred to at follow-up meetings and taken out again when progress is measured. They also reflect any plan changes that have to be made during the project's implementation. In a word, the *Write on the Wall* process results in action. I hope the following pages help to smooth the road that leads you to better project management.

SECTION 1: PREPLANNING

This section identifies the key components needed to conduct effective group planning meetings.

CHAPTER 1
Prepare To Plan

Some preparation must be completed before beginning any group planning process. This chapter explains the importance of preplanning and presents the steps to take to define a group's purpose and maintain its focus in order to achieve its goals.

The Group Mind

Write on the Wall is based on the premise that two or more heads are better than one. For years, research supported the theory that people react to the ideas of other group participants during simple brainstorming sessions. A dynamic experience seems to expand constructive thinking.

Several years ago, I was a member of a group trying to develop some new product ideas. Many of the members had worked independently without success. But when we participated collectively in a brainstorming session, we developed so many new ideas that they would have taken two lifetimes to put into effect.

Brainstorming sessions are often used for solving simple problems or larger ones such as developing advertising campaigns, and they are often conducted without much structure. But brainstorming can be expanded to create powerful strategic business plans—it is all a matter of technique. This book shows how a planning group can follow certain principles and processes to formulate a strategic business or marketing plan, advertising plan, and public relations plan.

Why Most Committees Don't Work

It is probably not an exaggeration to say that most committee meetings in the profit and nonprofit sectors are a waste of time, talent, and money. Committees' missions, or purposes, are often vague, and there may be little structure to the meetings. Even when there is an agenda and decisions are made, there is often a lack of follow-through or lack of a mechanism to put the decisions into effect. The following sections explain, step-by-step, how to correct these errors.

Steps To Achieving Focus

First, remember that group members can only work effectively together if they remain focused on what they decide to achieve collectively. The following steps can help build and maintain group focus.

1. Agree on a purpose. From the beginning, the group members must agree on what they have come together to accomplish—the **group purpose.** Defining the group purpose presents an opportunity for participatory planning. So get the group together, along with any key organizational people; conduct a brainstorming session; and discuss the group purpose. Throughout the discussions, write everyone's ideas down and develop consensus on what the group purpose and specific organizational issues are.

The first time I conducted a planning session for people who did not know each other very well, I could tell that it was going to be a difficult meeting. Some participants had come to the meeting with reservations about the process. Before starting the meeting, I asked everyone to introduce themselves and give their thoughts, concerns, and preliminary ideas on the subject that was being addressed.

Each idea or concern was written on a flipchart titled **Group Thoughts.** Then there was a discussion about the purpose of the planning group and the most appropriate meeting or planning format to accomplish the agreed-upon goal.

Therefore, before starting the actual planning, we took the time to get to know each other and put our thoughts, biases, concerns, and ideas on the table. We also developed consensus on why we were there and the planning process we would use. The participants left the meeting feeling good about developing a workable plan. From that experience, I learned to "warm up" a group, help the participants develop a focus, and agree on a purpose before starting any work.

2. Present the facts. Presenting the facts helps a group maintain its focus. There is nothing like hard evidence to move a discussion of a problem and its solution from stalemate to resolution. The processes of gathering background information and presenting it in a way that ensures the group never loses sight of its mission is key to the *Write on the Wall* process.

3. Choose a facilitator. An effective meeting **facilitator** extracts the pearls of wisdom from group discussions and keeps the group on track, so its members do not lose sight of their original purpose. To help maintain the group focus, the facilitator needs to know when to speak, when to listen, and what questions to ask to encourage group thinking.

4. Choose a plan format. At the beginning of the planning process, the group leader should work with the group to develop a **structured format.** The format should include the specific topics to discuss and the order in which to address them. These topics comprise the agenda of the planning meetings. The format varies depending on the type of plan that is needed. For example, strategic business plans, marketing plans, advertising plans, and public relations plans all have their own purposes—therefore, their own planning formats.

The type of plan to develop is not always obvious. I have seen more group planning projects fail because of the wrong type of plan format than for any other reason. So give a lot of thought to format prior to scheduling planning meetings. Sometimes it is helpful to have a small group attend a private planning session just to develop and agree on the best format for the plan.

I remember meeting with one particular planning group to discuss format. Most of the afternoon was spent developing what was thought to be an appropriate format. A few days later, one meeting participant said she and someone else had some problems with the plan format and how it applied to the issue being addressed. They felt that their supervisor had exerted undue influence on the format decision, and they were concerned that it was not going to result in an effective plan. Sharing their concern, I suggested a change to a somewhat different format during the next planning meeting. Everyone agreed to the change that produced a solid plan with which everyone felt comfortable.

This book presents some basic group planning formats. With experience, you can eventually adjust them to suit particular group planning situations. The key is flexibility.

5. Find a flipchart and a wall. I wrote an entire chapter about the effective use of a **flipchart and wall space,** the most useful tools to any group planning endeavor. Flipcharting meeting ideas and activities in a group planning session replaces the often inefficient act of recording meeting minutes. Taking minutes requires that a group member take notes of everything said in the meeting, organize the information after the meeting, and read it back at the beginning of the next group meeting. Aside from flipcharting being more accurate and less time-consuming, it is more logical to have facts and ideas displayed on the wall for reference purposes throughout the entire planning process.

Selecting Planning Group Participants

After the decision to use the group approach is made, select the appropriate individuals for the planning team. Who should be in the group and why are the most frequently asked questions when selecting participants. The answers to these questions really depend on the plan that needs to be developed, and who must implement it.

Some plans go deep into the organization, including division managers and supervisors—an excellent idea if you can manage it. In a smaller organization, identify who, other than the top two or three people, would contribute to such a process and carry out important parts of the plan. I have seen successful planning meetings held with as few as two participants and as many as 20 participants. The ideal situation involves six to 12 participants. Formats can be adjusted to accommodate any number, and larger groups can be broken up into smaller work groups.

Remember, a basic rule in group planning is to involve those who are primarily responsible for the plan's execution. They have the strongest sense of ownership. For example, in developing an advertising plan or a public relations plan—both of which follow a different format than a strategic business plan—it may not be necessary to involve an organization's senior management. But be sure to involve the organization's advertising or public relations agency. In fact, involving organizational advertising and public relation representatives even in basic business and marketing planning sessions is a smart move. People in these businesses are creative—a good quality to bring to a planning process.

Be sure to have some representation from the operational areas. These people can spot problematic strategies immediately. Invite one or two operational or procedural individuals to the group planning meeting. If this is not practical, meet with them before each session to get their input. Also report meeting results to them to get their reactions to proposed strategies. This will provide them with necessary background information when their groups are required to develop subsections of the overall plan. Some businesses even include customers in their planning groups, and many nonprofit organizations include clients.

The planning example used throughout the book is a **strategic business plan.** A strategic business plan usually consists of four components. First, a **mission statement** states the basic purposes of the company or organization. The plan also includes an overall **situation analysis** that identifies an organization's major problems and opportunities. The third component of a strategic business plan lists **goals and objectives.** These must be defined and agreed to by the planning group participants before any actions and responsibilities are assigned. Finally, depending on the organization's size, a **strategic action plan** that lists strategies and tactics and notes individual accountability is developed along divisional lines or by strategic area. Thus, the people who should be involved in a strategic business planning exercise include senior management and divisional heads who have major roles in the plan's strategies.

Group Conflicts

A good facilitator serves as an effective moderator when dealing with difficult personalities that surface during group planning exercises. Creativity is important, but is it necessary to put up with so-and-so's ridiculous ideas? Yes. In brainstorming, there is no such thing as a dumb idea. And no harm comes from discussing all ideas. Be willing to turn the world on its ear when embarking on a group planning project.

Remember that reason usually prevails. If facts are gathered up front, a good situation analysis can be developed. And with a thorough analysis, a plan will almost write itself despite the inevitable personality conflicts.

What seems to be a ridiculous notion at first might be workable when looked at from a different perspective. A so-called crazy idea modified intelligently might set an organization apart from its competitors. Remember that "there's gold in them thar heads." It does not do the group or the organization any good to leave it there.

Summary of Key Points

1. Brainstorming is an effective way for a group to identify key issues. Further, the group approach can be used effectively in business and organizational planning.

2. Planning groups must maintain focus to be successful.

3. Group focus can be achieved and maintained by
• defining the group purpose or mission
• basing arguments and course of action on facts
• choosing an effective facilitator to moderate meetings
• choosing an appropriate plan/meeting format
• using flipcharts and wall space to "build" the plan.

4. Planning group participants should include
• primary organizational stakeholders
• internal/external subject matter experts
• key personnel responsible for plan implementation.

CHAPTER 2
The Art of Facilitation

A group leader may not be the person conducting the meetings during the group planning process. In many cases, a meeting facilitator is selected to lead the group through the planning process. This chapter describes the role and responsibilities of the meeting facilitator.

Let's begin by describing what a meeting facilitator does not have to do. The facilitator is not responsible for scheduling meetings, doing preliminary meeting research, appointing the planning group members, or distributing meeting minutes or summaries. Nor is a meeting facilitator responsible for carrying out tasks or details of a meeting's resulting action plans.

However, there are situations where a facilitator may serve a dual role as a group planning member and be responsible for some or all of the above matters. But the only role a facilitator should have in a meeting is that of a mediator, helping the group work through its agenda.

Having a facilitator present does not absolve anyone in the planning group from doing what he or she normally does. For example, if a supervisor or committee chairperson uses a facilitator to run the planning meetings of his or her group, that supervisor or chairperson is still accountable for the success of the plan. No one should feel that his or her job is threatened because a facilitator runs a group planning meeting—whether the facilitator is a group member or not.

Role of the Facilitator

Now let us concentrate on a facilitator's roles and responsibilities. The facilitator must play a leading role by helping the group members decide what plan is needed. Is it a business plan, marketing plan, advertising plan, or public relations plan? He or she also directs the group through the agreed-upon meeting structure or plan format.

When the type of plan is agreed on, meet with the planning group, or its most important members, to review alternative formats and select—or develop—a format that seems most appropriate for the situation. Remember, there is no one rigid format for each type of plan.

One reward of facilitating group planning sessions is the satisfaction one gets in developing a new format or a new twist on an old format. The facilitator has an obligation to make sure the group is comfortable with the format, that the format makes sense, and that it works for the group. While some examples of planning formats are presented in this book, you also will be shown how appropriate changes can be made and where shortcuts can be taken when necessary.

Facilitator as Educator

When developing a planning format with the group, the facilitator provides a road map that shows how the major elements of the plan develop from start to finish. Thus, another role of the facilitator is that of educator.

Many planning groups are impatient for results. Those with little experience in planning, or at least group planning, may expect to develop a total plan by the end of the first session. The participants will be surprised and disappointed when all they have is a plan to plan, after spending several hours in a meeting. They may even be cynical about the prospects of the group actually developing a plan at all. For this reason, it is a good idea to begin the first planning meeting with an explanation of what the group is going to do and estimate how long it will take.

Even more important, get the group members' ideas and reservations on the table and address them. Document their concerns, thoughts, and suggestions on a flipchart during a Group Thoughts exercise which was explained earlier. Remember that this is a participatory process, so people should be encouraged to participate from the beginning.

After discussing the group's thoughts, start working on the selection of the format—that in itself is a great educational experience. When people work together on a planning format and know that they have some input into the development of the road map, they begin to think positively and develop some enthusiasm for the job they are about to do.

Preparation

A good facilitator is like a good athlete, musician, or comedian—the best ones make it look easy. But their excellent performances come only after much preparation, involving not only the experience of having done it before, but a lot of thought, study, and practice. One gets better at facilitating meetings with practice, but a facilitator never becomes so proficient that he or she does not have to prepare for meetings beforehand.

One of the best ways to prepare for a meeting is to go through the process and develop a possible plan format either alone or with another person. Anticipate problems and questions, and figure out how to address them. Actually write out a plan—maybe even more than one version—and keep it as a reference for the first meeting.

It is a good idea to have a "back-pocket" plan to refer to during those awkward moments of silence, when the group is not responding. Offer an idea from this plan when the group loses its momentum or focus. Even if the group members do not like a particular idea, their reactions to it will help keep the process moving. The final plan developed by the group may look nothing like the original outline, but the up-front preparation builds a facilitator's confidence.

Once I facilitated a planning session for a large company. The group was assigned the task of developing a plan for alternative methods of product distribution. One problem was that the group members came from distant places and only had three hours to complete the plan.

For several days, I worked on various plan formats and discussed them over the phone with the group leader. Then I spent several additional days writing out complete back-pocket plans so that I became familiar with many of the issues before the planning meeting. As it turned out, I got total agreement on both the major issues and the key planning steps within the first 30 minutes of the meeting. The group spent the rest of the time developing the strategies and tactics. Because of my preliminary meeting planning, I was even able to make suggestions in these areas. Preparation paid off and enabled the group to agree on and complete the plan within the three-hour time frame.

Know the Group

The last thing that a facilitator must do before a planning session is the same thing that any public speaker, stage actor, or entertainer has to do: Read the group. Learning as much as possible about the individuals in the group before the meeting will ease the overall group communications process. This knowledge also helps a facilitator draw people into the discussions based on their areas of expertise. Here are some ways to learn about group participants:

1. Learn about the group participants' backgrounds. Sometimes this can be done beforehand as part of the meeting preparation. Talk with people in the organization's personnel department or the group members' department heads to get a feel for what the group members do, what their interests might be, and what the members' roles might be in the group. One can even draw on past personal interactions with the members if he or she has worked with them before.

2. Identify the experts. When planning something technical and an expert is in the group, find out who he or she is. If a marketing plan is being developed and a well-trained, experienced marketing person is in the group, try to get this person's support and assistance. Recognizing the experts in the group is good politics and good planning.

If learning about the group members in advance is not possible, get to know them as much as possible at the meeting itself. A good way to do this is through the Group Thoughts exercise explained on page 6.

When To Speak and When To Listen

A facilitator should enlist the support and participation of *all* the members throughout each meeting. Along with this task, the facilitator is responsible for monitoring any domineering or nonchalant personalities on the team.

What can be done with a "bully," talker, or wallflower? First and foremost, treat everyone with equal respect. Second, make certain that everyone gets a chance to speak. If someone is quiet, periodically ask him or her a question. If someone is a bully or talker, let this person speak and then politely but firmly remind him or her that this is a participatory process in which everyone needs to be heard.

There are some techniques for dealing with situations where one or two people persist in disturbing the process. One technique involves conducting a round-robin discussion on each issue, setting a ground rule that no one speaks again until everyone has been heard. Another technique is to have people write out their thoughts on cards. After all the group members' thoughts are recorded, the facilitator reads them aloud and leads the subsequent discussion.

It also is crucial for a facilitator to develop strong listening skills.

Too much input from a facilitator can stifle a group's creative progress, so learn to interject only when the discussion stops or steers off course. Ask more questions and give fewer opinions. The facilitator's major objective should be to get the group's members to do the talking and arrive at a consensus. The facilitator is like the conductor of an orchestra—he or she is an important player, but the group's members, like the orchestra's musicians, should "make the music."

Flexibility

Another asset a facilitator must maintain is flexibility. For example, the very best planning format or agenda may have been developed but here it is, one hour into a scheduled three-hour meeting, the group is already behind schedule, and two participants announce that they need to leave in an hour because of an unforeseen emergency. This is a common occurrence at group planning sessions. In some cases, another meeting can and should be scheduled. However, this is often not practical or even possible. In such cases, learn to be flexible and short-cut the process or agenda while maintaining the basic integrity of the plan. Some examples of shortcuts will be noted throughout the discussion of the basic planning steps addressed in subsequent chapters.

Being a facilitator is not always easy, but it can be a challenging, creative, and rewarding experience. When a good plan comes out of the process, it can make a facilitator feel like a proud parent.

Summary of Key Points

1. The primary responsibilities of a meeting facilitator are to
- explain his or her role
- develop group consensus about meeting purpose
- understand group participants' strengths/weaknesses
- ensure everyone has a chance to participate
- help the group stay focused on desired outcomes
- offer suggestions on how to proceed
- maintain meeting/plan flexibility.

2. A facilitator's meeting preparation should include
- developing possible plan formats
- learning about group participants
- surveying the meeting location/conditions.

CHAPTER 3
Create a Plan

The *World Book Dictionary* defines the word **plan** as "a way of making or doing something that has been worked out beforehand." It is hard to imagine anything of value being accomplished without a plan. However, many businesses and nonprofit enterprises go on day after day—year after year—without a plan, because their activities are based solely on reactions to customers, voters, members, or other outside environmental influences. Some organizations are starting to take a different view of the act of planning. A combination of factors is changing the way many organizations conduct their business. This chapter explores the importance of planning and outlines the components of a basic strategic business plan.

Reasons To Formulate a Plan

First, competitors are devoting more time to planning their long-term strategies. Voters and key stakeholders are becoming more visible and vocal within organizations. Members also are becoming more concerned with the positions their organizations take on key issues, and customers demand that the latest goods and services be made available sooner.

Planning provides a perfect opportunity for organizations to communicate with their customers or managers to get their input in advance, instead of just reacting to circumstances as they occur. It also provides an opportunity for organizations to fulfill their employees' needs for active involvement in the company's success. Group planning enhances empowerment and shows employees that their ideas and opinions really count. In a nutshell, planning helps groups manage change instead of being managed by it.

Planning Versus the Plan Itself

While a developed plan of action is a key asset to have, the *act* of planning—the creation process—may be even more important than the plan itself, because group planning is key in developing teamwork. Even if the plan that results from the effort is less than ideal, an organization will be significantly stronger and more effective because it used the group approach to planning.

Types of Plans

First of all, an organization should have a basic strategic business plan that covers a period of at least three years. This basic, long-range plan should be updated annually and serves as the springboard for other plans that address such issues as budgeting, product development, advertising, public relations, and internal and external communications. A strategic business plan is important because it forces an organization to face basic issues. Usually, this type of plan includes several distinct elements. The first element of a strategic business plan is the mission statement—the definition of the purpose of the organization. Next, the plan documents the current economic, market, and competitive situation of the overall industry and within the organization specifically. A strategic business plan also identifies an organization's problems and opportunities through a thorough situation analysis and sets overall goals.

All of the elements should be created within a group setting. After identifying the major issues, the planning team should then develop objectives and strategies around each of the issues. These issue-oriented plans will spawn other plans.

Getting Started—The Hardest Part

Sometimes group planning must be conducted despite the lack of a finalized strategic business plan. For example, a crisis communications plan needs to be developed immediately, with no time to wait for the completion of a long-range plan. This is not the best situation, but it can happen. In such cases, a plan can be developed based on some general assumptions and then altered, if necessary, after the long-range plan is completed. This is the kind of flexibility that is needed in the group planning process. At times, plans may seem like nothing more than plans to plan. That's fine! Planning is a dynamic activity—one thing does invariably lead to another. For example, when planning to visit a friend in a distant country, first determine how to get to the country. Once in the country, plan how to get to your friend's city. A street map may then be needed to get to the friend's house.

If an organization does its homework and develops a long-range strategic business plan around major issues, the plan can become a road map for teams that are formed to develop smaller plans. Planning is similar to writing a term paper, book, or letter. Do not wait around for inspiration or the right moment—just start it. To begin group planning, appoint a facilitator, call a meeting (initially of the top people), pick a format similar to the ones described in this book, start the process, and see how it goes.

Avoid Dust-Gatherers

Do not be surprised if someone shows up at the first group meeting with a dusty, old, 12-inch-thick portfolio labeled, "Long-Range Plan." Office shelves and desk drawers all over the United States are full of thick, dusty plans with life spans of about a week. Because these plans rarely ever see sunlight after development, many people are cynical about the importance of planning and consider it a great waste of time and money.

In my opinion, most classic dust-gatherers are too long, too complicated, and not developed by the organizations but imposed on them from outside sources. Furthermore, many lack an action plan—the vital component that outlines who is to do what by when.

There is nothing more frustrating and demoralizing for a group than to receive a thick, complicated document and hear "put it into effect." It makes much more sense to develop the plan in stages, moving from the general to the specific. What I suggest is an action-oriented planning system. The organization itself creates a strategic business plan, and the supporting documents are simple and directional. Subplans spawned from this overall plan may get technical and detailed, but the basic strategic business plan does not.

The End Is Just the Beginning

The most important part of a plan is the end. This is where the action plan is, which specifies who is responsible for doing what by when. Without an action plan, you have a study instead of a plan. In the group approach to planning, the participants themselves commit to what they can do and by when. If a plan has an action plan and regularly scheduled follow-ups through meetings and reports, it will not gather dust on shelves—it will be referred to continually as the group members complete their self-assigned tasks.

Summary of Key Points

1. A group planning process must be documented by a written plan. Oral communication is not adequate.

2. Plans must be created and agreed to by all members of the group who are responsible for their implementation.

3. Don't wait for the right moment; get started.

4. A long-range strategic plan is the springboard for other plans.

5. The action plan is the most important part of the plan.

CHAPTER 4
Face the Wall, Please

One of my first observations when I started conducting group planning sessions was the apparent need of people to focus their eyes on something during the meeting. This focus point should be the recorded progress of the plan on a flipchart and displayed on a wall in full view. This chapter explains how to use the flipchart and wall to help maintain optimal group focus on the task at hand.

When a flipchart is blank and no paper is taped to the wall, planning participants invariably fumble through files or doodle on note pads. If someone is speaking to the group, it is likely that a significant number of the participants will not really be paying attention. On the other hand, when material is written and displayed on the wall, people's eyes focus on it as they speak and as they listen to others.

Watching the Plan Develop

There is something psychologically comforting about looking at the plan on the wall as the group develops it. The wall almost becomes a group meditation device that helps clear the participants' minds, helps them focus on the issue, and helps to bond the group together. The wall, in a sense, becomes the group's mind. In other words, the device makes it possible for a group to function as one.

Perhaps the biggest advantage to writing on the wall is immediacy. Planning participants can refer back to ideas and decisions at any time during the meeting, which enables them to challenge the wording of the plan as it is written. This is possible because the group facilitator writes out each idea, fact, and decision on flipchart sheets and displays them on the wall in sequential order.

You might consider recruiting a separate recorder who can print legibly to document the meeting, so the facilitator is free to run the meeting. When in doubt about what to write, ask the contributor of the idea to restate the point. Then read it aloud to ensure correctness. After recording each item, write the number of the next one and then leave space. This encourages thinking and helps the group to move on to the next idea.

Another advantage to using the wall to record your planning meeting is the joy people get from seeing their plan develop before their eyes. Similar to a sports team watching a winning score develop, it becomes the focus of the players' attention. It becomes the "product" they are building together; therefore, it creates a spirit of teamwork that is necessary to the success of any group endeavor.

Many times I have seen groups cheer at the end of a planning session after they look at what they have accomplished. Even when they do not cheer, they usually sit for a moment and gaze almost lovingly at this "creation" on the wall—similar to an artist contemplating with satisfaction the painting that he or she just completed.

Selecting an Appropriate Planning Room

At this point, you may wonder where to find enough wall space to employ the *Write on the Wall* technique. Take this issue into consideration when you plan such a meeting. Some rooms are better adapted to the process than others. For example, some wall surfaces can hold transparent plastic tape, while other surfaces require the use of masking tape only. Still others will not hold anything because the owner of the wall will not let you affix anything to it. Find a room with enough usable wall (or window) space, so you can display many flipchart sheets in plain view of the meeting participants. Also have the right size room in order to display flipchart sheets close enough to the people so they can read what is written.

Maximizing the Use of Wall Space

There are two basic ways you can use the wall for a *Write on the Wall* session. You can tape blank flipchart sheets to the wall in advance, and fill them up as the meeting progresses. Another way to use available space is to tape flipchart sheets to the wall as they are completed during the meeting. The method you choose may be dictated by the room's layout, but there are distinct advantages to using an easel to record the meeting's progression. First, group members do not have to move during the meeting so that the recorder can write. They can basically maintain their position and just look around when they want to check on something taped to the wall. You also have the advantage of being able to pin the completed sheets to curtains or over pictures on the wall because you do not need a hard surface on which to write. Finally, the recorder is less likely to damage the wall with markers if an easel is used.

On the other hand, there is something psychologically challenging about walking into a room and seeing the walls covered with blank paper. It gives the group members an effective visual image of what they are about to do. It also saves time during the meeting, because you do not have to stop after each sheet is completed to tape it to the wall. A word of warning: If you write on sheets taped to the wall, be sure to use a double or triple layer of paper so that the marker ink does not damage the wall.

Supplies To Stock

The supplies that are needed for a *Write on the Wall* session include a flipchart and easel, felt-tipped markers, and masking tape. When purchasing felt-tipped markers, look for ones without a strong chemical odor. Otherwise, you may feel light-headed after writing for an extended period of time. Black or dark blue markers are preferable for writing, because they are highly visible colors. A red marker is suitable for under-lining or highlighting key points.

Summary of Key Points

Although writing on a flipchart sounds fairly straightforward, a few basic rules of thumb can make the recording process run more smoothly and efficiently.

1. Always print in block letters. Script is difficult to read.

2. Keep sentences short.

3. Use an outline format, using numbers and letters.

4. Use easy-to-read black or blue felt-tipped markers. These colors are easily seen from a distance.

5. Number each sheet of paper so proper sequencing is maintained when notes are typed.

6. Learn to print fast. This comes with practice.

7. You might consider recruiting a separate recorder who can print legibly to document the meeting, so the facilitator is free to run the meeting.

CHAPTER 5
First Things First

Many people either question the need for planning or have no patience for the planning process—especially a group planning process. This issue needs to be addressed in your opening group session. But before you call your first group planning meeting, meet with some key organizational people—some of whom may end up in your planning group—and have an open, honest discussion about the need for planning.

Setting the Stage for Success

This precursory meeting is an excellent way to accomplish several tasks before the group planning process actually begins. It also helps to find out who supports the planning process and who is against it. The knowledge gained through this exercise can also help the group leader and meeting facilitator to deal patiently with unwilling participants.

Even if some participants in this meeting do not fully support the idea that planning is important or some participants do not completely buy-in to the particular planning process that will be recommended to the actual planning group, all participants should agree on why they are meeting and what they hope to accomplish. Will the group be working to clarify the organization's overall direction? Is there a problem with a specific product? Is the problem a communications or public relations issue? Getting agreement on the issue to address in the group planning process is imperative to choosing an appropriate plan format and choosing the right planners.

Choosing the Plan Format

After establishing the issue, the group needs to determine what type of plan format should be recommended to the group planning team.

When choosing a plan format, address the easy choices first. If the issue is how to advertise a product, service, or event, then develop an advertising plan (see chapter 13). If media publicity is necessary or an organization is interested in presenting a favorable image to its publics, then a public relations plan is probably most appropriate (see chapter 14).

The two plan formats used as examples throughout most of this book are marketing plan formats, which are used most often to develop strategic business plans and product development plans. Sometimes organizations also have corresponding annual plans that are based on the strategic business plan but also include annual budget information. Such long-range and annual plans can be developed for the whole organization, each of its major divisions, or a combination of both.

The marketing process is "the managerial process of identifying, analyzing, choosing, and exploiting marketing opportunities to fulfill the company's mission and objectives."[1] In other words, marketing is considered the business you are in, and everything in your organization must support it.

Strategic Business Plan Formats

If you choose the marketing approach to strategic business planning, start by developing a mission statement that answers the following question: "What is the purpose of this organization?" Following the development of a mission statement, organize a straightforward planning approach that includes the following steps:

1. Gather the necessary background information.
2. Develop a situation analysis of the organization.
3. Identify major problems and opportunities.
4. Agree on the goals and objectives that must be achieved.
5. Create the strategies and tactics that help to achieve the defined goals and objectives.

Analyzing the Market

One of the most important tasks for a planning group developing a strategic business plan is to analyze how the economy is affecting the overall business. Next, define a company's targeted customer base through **market segmentation,** and examine the **marketing mix** of the organization and its competitors. The marketing mix—sometimes

[1]Kotler, Philip, *Principles of Marketing.* Englewood Cliffs, NJ: Prentice-Hall, 1980, p. 89.

referred to as the **four "Ps"**— includes "the particular blend of controllable marketing variables that the [organization] uses to achieve its objective in the target market."[2] The four Ps are the product, price, place (distribution), and promotion of an organization. The elements of the marketing mix are defined as follows.

■ **Product** covers the development and execution of products, services, or events, as well as their features, benefits, and performance.

■ **Price** covers pricing history, rationale, and profitability.

■ **Place,** or distribution, includes all the steps between product production and purchase by the customer (i.e., warehousing, middlemen, and sales).

■ **Promotion** includes advertising, mailings, and publicity.

You may want to have a separate category for sales and service, or include sales promotion in either distribution or promotion—the choice is up to you. The same applies to areas such as manufacturing and human resources. You may want to have separate categories for them or include them, as appropriate, under product or place.

The four Ps should be considered during each of the five planning steps listed above. Imagine putting the total plan on a matrix with the planning process steps listed down the vertical axis and the four Ps listed across the horizontal axis.

Suppose an organization's strategic business plan calls for the development of a new product or the development of detailed plans for each product or product line. The format used for the product plans essentially would be the same as that used for the overall plan—the marketing format.

Plan Format Options

After reading this book, you can decide which of the following two marketing plan formats fit your situation. The two plan outlines on page 28 list the steps to take. Option A works for simpler plans such as projects, small businesses, departments, products, or associations. Option B may be needed if you are developing an overall strategic business plan.

Assuming that an organization is committed to basing its decisions on what its target markets want and need, then it is a marketing-oriented organization, regardless of which planning format is selected. A marketing process begins when an organization starts "listening" to its customers' wants and needs. It continues with an analysis of customer

[2]Kotler, Philip, *Principles of Marketing*. Englewood Cliffs, NJ: Prentice-Hall, 1980, p. 89.

response, subsequent development of goods or services that meet customers' needs and wants, delivery of the goods or services to the market, and communication with the market that lets customers know about the goods or services. This cycle ends with listening again for the market's response and making any appropriate changes.

Sample Marketing Plan Formats

Option A

1. Develop a mission statement.
2. Determine informational needs.
3. Develop a situation analysis, considering marketing mix.
4. Identify problems and opportunities.
5. Set organizational goals.
6. Set objectives relative to problems and opportunities.
7. Develop strategies for achieving the objectives and goals.
8. Develop an action plan that defines who completes each strategy's tactics by an agreed-upon time.

Option B

1. Develop a mission statement.
2. Determine informational needs.
3. Develop a situation analysis, considering marketing mix.
4. Identify problems and opportunities.
5. Set organizational goals.
6. Identify major issue areas for planning—usually categories under which problems and opportunities can be grouped (e.g., product lines, product development, human resources, and operations). You may want to write short statements summarizing the problems and opportunities in each particular issue area.
7. Set objectives for each issue area (i.e., the results you need to achieve relative to the problems and opportunities within each issue area in order to achieve organizational goals).
8. Assign teams of planners to develop a plan for each issue area .
9. The teams then conduct group planning sessions to develop appropriate strategies and action plans for achieving the objectives in each issue area.

The planning process and formats can help you perfect a marketing orientation. And it will help to ensure an organization's longevity—the ability to meet the needs of its market or constituents better than the competition and do it at a profit. Planning is a means to that end.

Selecting the Planners and Facilitator

Now that the type of plan and plan format are determined, consider who should be in the planning group. As stated earlier, the people doing the planning should be those who have the major responsibility for carrying it out. As the plan is not yet developed, you will have to make some guesses as to whom this might be.

In my many years of leading planning groups, I have never found this to be a major problem. You probably have an idea which departments or committees need to be involved in the plan, so the heads of the areas should be invited to participate along with an associate for back-up.

As the planning process works its way through an organization, and new groups are formed to develop pieces of the overall plan or subplans, more individuals will get involved. For example, a strategic business plan may call for the development of a new product; then product managers and others will team up to develop a product plan. The product plan may call for the development of an advertising plan; then an organization's advertising or marketing experts will get involved. All the planning steps give an organization the opportunity to involve more people, and each step creates an opportunity for input from the rank and file.

What is the ideal number of people in a planning group? As stated earlier, great plans have been developed by as few as two people and as many as 20 people. The ideal is probably somewhere between six and 12 members.

Who should be the facilitator? Chapter 2 described the qualities needed to be a good facilitator—preparedness, flexibility, and the ability to know and read a group. Select a facilitator carefully. Ideally, he or she will be the principal planning developer in your organization.

The last thing to do before your first meeting is select and reserve the meeting room, keeping in mind the features mentioned in chapter 4. The group leader or facilitator should become familiar with the room, and know from personal inspection that it meets the standards for a *Write on the Wall* planning session. Study the room and decide whether to work from an easel or blank flipchart paper taped on the walls.

Now you are ready to move on to the first planning meeting.

Summary of Key Points

1. Conduct a preliminary meeting of key planning individuals to
- define the planning group's purpose
- map out a tentative planning format (see examples)
- commit to becoming a marketing-oriented organization
- identify potential group participants
- identify a potential meeting facilitator.

2. Select the appropriate planning group participants.

3. Select the appropriate meeting room that will accommodate the *Write on the Wall* planning session.

SECTION 2: GROUP PLANNING MEETINGS

The next five chapters provide step-by-step instructions on how to organize and run group planning sessions that produce action-oriented plans.

CHAPTER 6
Meeting 1: Missions and Purposes Defined

The planning group members assemble for the first meeting. Some are more enthusiastic than others. Some appear to be present only because their bosses ordered them to attend. There will always be different levels of dedication for the process. Remember that many people are won over to group planning only by gaining firsthand experience with the process.

Warm-ups

As previously mentioned in chapter 2, get to know the individuals through a Group Thoughts exercise. In addition, if the group is unfamiliar with the planning process, provide them with a brief run-down of the basic steps.

After compiling a Group Thoughts list, tape it to the wall in the back of the room, and suggest that the group revisit the list at the end of the meeting or planning process. The reason for revisiting the list is to make sure that all the group's initial thoughts were addressed during the meeting. If any thoughts or concerns were not addressed, this would be the time to make the appropriate changes or additions to the plan to cover the ideas. Explain this as part of the process ground rules at the beginning of the meeting. It will go a long way to increase the participants' comfort levels and improve the level of participation.

Define Missions/Purposes

After completing the warm-up phase, address missions and purposes. State the organization's mission, and clarify the purposes of the planning group, as well as the purpose of this particular meeting. Write these clarifying statements on flipchart sheets and hang them on the wall, so group members can refer to them often during the session. I recommend clarifying and writing out the purpose of every meeting because there are often different opinions among a group about the meeting's purpose. If the group members do not agree on the purpose of each meeting up front, it is difficult to stay on track. These preliminary statements should begin with the following words:

■ The purpose of our organization is to...(state the mission).

■ The purpose of this planning group is to...(state the group purpose).

■ The purpose of this meeting is to...(define what the group needs to accomplish by the end of the meeting.)

For example, the mission of one organization might be to meet the need for quality recreational exercise equipment, provide meaningful employment to its employees, and provide a generous return to its owners. Or in the case of a nonprofit organization, the mission might be to meet the needs of the mentally ill in its community and provide a rewarding experience to staff, volunteers, and board members. And the purpose of the planning process is to develop a strategic business plan for the organization. Then the purpose of the meeting could be to develop a situation analysis. Whatever the purposes are, the group members must agree, and the purposes must be written out and displayed during the meeting.

Do not fall into the trap of stating that the sole purpose of your business is making money. While making money may be included in the purpose, it is not the whole purpose and can usually be covered under goals. An organization's purpose or mission should be written from the perspective of the needs of the community, market, owners, and employees. After all, only by meeting the needs of people can an organization be successful, financially or otherwise.

When everyone agrees on the organization's mission and the group's purpose, review the type of plan and the recommended planning format. Then open the floor for discussion, address all concerns and ideas, and build a consensus for the proposed format before proceeding. The group should feel comfortable with the format. Remember, the format recommended was decided during the preplanning meeting described in the previous chapter.

Ask Questions/Seek Answers

Most of the first meeting should consist of identifying the information or data the group needs in order to proceed with the planning process. Therefore, it is important to get the group to agree that it should assess its needs during the first meeting. In some cases, you may not have time to devote an entire meeting to just determining informational needs, or you may feel confident that the group already has most of the information it needs. If this is the case, the group may opt to shorten or even eliminate this step. Usually, this is left up to the meeting facilitator and the group. But good information is critical to good planning, and more often than not it takes some time to gather and analyze this information. A plan based on erroneous information could be more dangerous than not having a plan at all. The following checklist can help to determine information needs.

Information Needs Assessment Questionnaire

Product/Service/Event

■ What is the organization's market share? What are the major competitors' market shares? (These may be published numbers, or you may have to conduct market research.)

■ What is happening to the market? (If the market is declining, it may be unwise to invest much effort into a product.)

■ How do the current product features and benefits compare with the competitors'?

■ How do customers or the market rate the product(s) versus those of the competitors?

■ What's new in the market? What are the trends?

■ What are the needs and wants of the target market? How are these needs and wants being met? How well are the competitors meeting their customers' wants and needs?

■ What can be done to meet customers' wants and needs better?

Price

■ How does current pricing compare with that of the competitors?

■ What is the organization's pricing history? What is the pricing history of the competitors? Do either have a relationship to market share history?

■ Is current pricing profitable?

■ How price-sensitive is the consumer?

■ What are the organization's pricing objectives? Have these objectives been achieved?

Information Needs Assessment Questionnaire (continued)

Place (Distribution)

■ What are the current channels of distribution? Are they successful? How do they compare with the competitors'?

■ How effective is the sales force? Are salespeople meeting their goals? Are overall sales goals being met?

■ What new distribution methods should be considered?

■ What is the current level of customer service satisfaction?

Promotion

■ How successful is current advertising? How successful are the competitors'? Has advertising awareness research been conducted?

■ What merchandising is being done? Is it successful?

■ What is spent for advertising versus competitors' costs?

Other

■ What is the economic outlook? How might it affect business?

■ Are there any current production problems?

■ Is the most up-to-date technology currently used?

■ What are current employee competence and morale levels?

■ How does the organization's current image compare to its competitors'?

■ What are the regulatory issues?

Even if you have limited time to gather information, you still need to ask the basic question: What do we need to know about ourselves, our environment, our markets, and our competitors to develop this plan? As previously stated, marketing and strategic business planning should address products, services, or events; pricing; place or distribution and sales; and promotion/advertising in each of its steps. This provides a clue as to what you need to know. Once this is determined, ask if the answers to these questions are available? If not, determine how to get them and who is going to do it?

The list of questions on the information needs assessment is not intended to be complete, and many of them may not even be applicable to your organization. They simply show the kind of exercise that must be done to assess the information that is needed to develop a situation analysis, which is the next step in the planning process.

Regardless of how the research is completed and by whom, the following research matrix can help develop the information needs of the group.

Figure 1: Research Matrix

	Questions	Answers				
		Have	Don't Have	Where to Get Answers	Who Will Get Answers	Deadlines
Products (Ours & Major Competitors)						
Price (Ours & Major Competitors)						
Place or Distribution (Ours & Major Competitors)						
Promotion (Ours & Major Competitors)						
Other						

While this matrix may apply more to a business than a nonprofit organization, it can be adapted for nonprofit use. In any case, the planning group members decide which categories best fit their current situation.

First Action Plan: Who Supplies What by When

Completing a research matrix also helps the group develop an action plan for this step in the planning process. An action plan states who is responsible for doing what by when. Never conclude a meeting without an action plan. In this case, the matrix automatically creates an action plan for gathering information or data.

While every meeting should end with an action plan, these "intermediate" action plans should not be incorporated in the final documented plan. They are used only to define what needs to be accomplished from one meeting to the next. The final plan should have its own action plan, which assigns responsibility for each of the tactics needed to complete each of the strategies.

Determine Strengths and Weaknesses

A planning group can do one more exercise during this meeting if it has the information. Using the matrix shown in Figure 2, the group can identify the organization's strengths and weaknesses, and compare them to the competition. If, on the other hand, more information must be gathered, this matrix can be completed at the next meeting.

Figure 2: Strengths and Weaknesses Matrix

	Product	Price	Place or Distribution	Production	Promotion
Competitor A	0	0	–	–	0
Competitor B	0	0	–	–	0

Code: + Better Than Competitors
              – Not As Good As Competitors

Based on the knowledge and the information on the marketing mix four Ps, compare the organization's performance to that of each of its major competitors. Use a plus sign (+) to indicate which areas the organization surpasses the competition, and a minus sign (-) to indicate areas that need improvement. Mark a zero (0) in the categories where there is no appreciable difference.

The matrix can be handed out to the group members for them to complete independently. If so, make sure that there is time to discuss the input and vote for a final selection of pluses and minuses. If the exercise is done collectively, try to develop a consensus on the ratings, and mark the appropriate responses on the matrix. In either case, complete the final official matrix on a large flipchart and tape it to the wall. This kind of exercise encourages active participation and provides invaluable information for the upcoming situation analysis.

Gather Information

A good way to find information and generate new ideas is to go to an organization's employees, customers, non-customers, members, shareholders, the community-at-large, or a particular segment of the market.

Some organizations tap this knowledge through **focus groups.** These are simply small groups of people who represent one of the groups mentioned above. Under the guidance of a leader or meeting facilitator, focus group participants are encouraged to engage in open discussion of the topic. The facilitator usually opens the discussion by asking some lead-in questions that are developed prior to the meeting. The questions might be written on a flipchart or poster cards. Someone usually records the major points brought up by the group, or the discussion is recorded so it can be heard in its entirety later.

While focus groups are frequently used to gather information, be aware of how the findings are interpreted. The information provided does not have any statistical validity because the group is too small. Focus groups, therefore, are best used to uncover issues that can be researched through more formal means, such as mailed questionnaires or telephone interviews, directed at a larger, more statistically valid number of people.

State, federal, and municipal governments, as well as trade associations, are often excellent sources of published data, such as demographic trends, sales trends, market share trends, and economic forecasts. Contact these sources to find out what they have available.

If your organization can hire a researcher or use an outside research company, I recommend it. Research can often be technical and sophisticated, and it is important to have valid information on which to base plans.

Closing the First Session

The last thing that must be done at the end of each meeting is to schedule the next one. Also remember that after this and every meeting, all planning group members should receive typed versions of what was recorded on the wall—especially the action plan. This will remind the participants of the assignments that must be completed before the next meeting.

Summary of Key Points

1. Begin the first planning meeting with a warm-up exercise that helps identify the general thoughts of group participants.

2. Define the organization's mission, the group's purpose, and the purpose of the meeting. Build consensus on what planning format should be used.

3. Prepare a research matrix that illustrates the group's informational needs and notes who is responsible for getting it by the next meeting.

4. Create an intermediate action plan that defines who will take what actions before the next meeting.

5. Prepare a strengths/weaknesses matrix to compare the organization to its competitors (if possible).

6. Schedule the next meeting, and distribute typed versions of the flipchart information and action plan.

CHAPTER 7
Meeting 2: Situation Analysis

Organizational planning cannot be done without a thorough analysis of the current situation. Every decision made should be based, at least in part, on the current problems and opportunities of an organization and its environment. A situation analysis is a picture of things as they are. The picture could also include how things were in the past and how they might be in the future if changes do not occur.

In group planning, the situation analysis is the springboard from which most of a plan will be developed. It should provide all the answers to the questions raised in the first meeting, addressing all the pertinent aspects of the four Ps and the strengths and weaknesses of the organization and its competitors.

Organize the Information

Develop a situation analysis by writing down and organizing the group's known facts and observations in outline form on flipchart paper to describe the current situation. Take your time in developing the situation analysis, because when this step is done well, the rest of the plan almost writes itself. Often times, I found groups spending more time developing the situation analysis than creating strategies—these were usually the best plans.

First, return to the matrix created to determine information needs. The most efficient way to analyze the information is to get the researchers to prepare written summaries of the key factors. Without this step, the group may waste valuable meeting time poring over details. Or send the summaries with the details attached to the group members before the meeting, so they can digest the information before using it to develop the situation analysis. It is vital that everyone look at the same information. It is easier to achieve group focus, if all group members look at the same data.

Decide What's Important

When developing a situation analysis, look at all the information carefully. In a way, it is similar to looking for clues. List all items that point to a possible problem or opportunity. Strategic business plans and marketing plans should focus on areas such as market share trends, product or service developments, technological changes, pricing trends, customer satisfaction, advertising effectiveness, sales trends, and other approporate areas, such as human resources.

And remember to keep your sentences short. While back-up statistics may be voluminous, try to avoid cluttering the analysis with verbose phrases. Instead, use a series of short phrases that summarize the information analyzed.

Also, do not forget to consider the insights and personal experiences of the people in the planning group when completing the analysis. The different points of view and the larger base of knowledge from group participants are two important benefits from using this planning approach. While the following examples are simplistic, they illustrate what a situation analysis might look like for a business or a nonprofit organization.

Situation Analysis (Business)

1. Our market share has remained steady for the past three years—currently in third place with 10 percent of the market.
2. The overall market is growing. It shows promise of continued growth during the next several years, especially within the 55-year-and-older segment.
3. Major competitors are organization X in first place in the market and organization Y in second place. Their market share trends are also holding steady.
4. Research indicates that the market sees little difference between the three organizations' products.
5. Product prices are virtually the same for all three organizations.
6. Our current production and distribution processes are out-dated and costly.
7. Our current profit margin is relatively low, which allows little room for price modifications.
8. Research indicates that some consumer needs are not met by any products—particularly the 55-year-and-older market segment.
9. Research indicates a lack of advertising awareness for any major competitor.
10. Research shows that our organizations's current customer service level is ranked fifth overall and dropping.
11. The rate of employee turnover is higher than the industry average.

Situation Analysis (Nonprofit)

1. Our organization is the major provider of services to the community's mentally-ill.
2. Until two years ago, it was the only provider of these service.
3. Within the past two years, two other groups started competing with us for state and federal funding.
4. The need for such services is growing beyond the capacity of all three organizations.
5. Our major fund-raising event has reached a plateau in its ability to raise funds.
6. State and federal dollars are not increasing.
7. The community at-large and the business community are not aware of mental health needs and what this organization does.
8. Mental illness among teenagers is growing, and no organization in the community addresses it.
9. Parents, teachers, and school principals do not know what to do when faced with teenage mental illness.
10. None of the organizations appeal directly to the community for financial help.

When the situation analysis is completed, there might be three or four items on one flipchart sheet; or many items, on 10 or more sheets. Over the years, I found that the average situation analysis runs about three flipchart sheets with about 10 to 15 items.

Identify Problems and Opportunities

After completing a situation analysis, identify the major organizational problems and opportunities that the planning group should address. Agreement on these areas is crucial because the group must ultimately develop strategies and tactics to solve the problems, take advantage of the opportunities, and achieve its overall goals and objectives.

In some cases, the problems and opportunities identified may be either too numerous or too complicated for the current planning group to address. With such cases, list the problems and opportunities under separate issue categories such as product or system, and assign those issue categories to subgroups to develop specific objectives, strategies, and tactics.

To prioritize the identified problems and opportunities, have the group members rate the items on a scale of 1 to 5 from least to most important. After each member prioritizes the items, the facilitator can either take a vote to rank the most important problems and opportunities, figure an average based on individual ratings, or seek a verbal consensus. After each problem and opportunity is rated, the group may decide to deal only with those rated above a certain level. This is a judgment call that depends on the available resources of the group to deal with the problems and opportunities. Review the previous example of a business situation analysis. Notice how the following list of problems and opportunities relate to the data collected.

Problems and Opportunities (Business)

1. Problem: Production and distribution processes are outdated and costly.
Opportunity: Solving this problem would increase profit margins and possibly create more options for competitive pricing.

2. Opportunity: Meet the needs of the 55-year-and-older market segment.

3. Opportunity: Establish a unique image for our business and its products.

4. Problem: Customer service levels are unacceptably low.
Opportunity: Implement ways to increase customer satisfaction and measure results.

5. Problem: Employee turnover is unacceptably high.
Opportunity: Reducing turnover will improve morale and customer service.

The problems and opportunities for the nonprofit example might look like this.

Problems and Opportunities (Nonprofit)

1. Problem: The organization's funding sources are diminishing, while the problem of mental illness is increasing.
Opportunity: Appeal for financial support.

2. Problem: No one addresses the teenagers' needs. Parents, teachers, and principals do not know where to get help.
Opportunity: Develop an awareness of our services among parents, teachers, and secondary school officials.

Oftentimes problems and opportunities are adequately identified in the situation analysis, so it is not necessary to write them out separately. When pressed for time, the facilitator may want to put a "P" or "O" next to the items in the situation analysis that represent major problems and opportunities. Just remember to be flexible and practical.

After completing a situation analysis and identifying the major problems and opportunities, close the planning meeting by scheduling the next one. Remember to distribute an action plan that notes any tasks that must be completed before the next session. At the next meeting, the group will take the next step in the planning process—setting goals and objectives.

Summary of Key Points

1. Analyze research data gathered prior to the meeting, and decide the most important areas on which to concentrate.

2. Develop a situation analysis that identifies the organization's and its competitors' current market positions.

3. Identify the problems and opportunities as described in the situation analysis.

4. Prioritize the most important problems and opportunities that need to be addressed by voting, calculating an average, or building a consensus.

5. Decide which problems and opportunities can be addressed by the group and which ones must be passed on to subgroups.

6. Schedule a meeting to develop group goals and objectives.

7. Distribute copies of the situation analysis and the list of problems and opportunities to each group member before the next meeting.

8. Note any actions that must be completed before the next meeting.

CHAPTER 8
Meeting 3: Goals and Objectives

R emember that the planning group's purpose is to develop an over-all strategic business plan using the marketing plan format. The flipcharts posted so far include the following:

- Group Thoughts
- Mission Statement of the Organization
- Purpose of the Planning Group
- Purposes of the Meetings
- Research Matrix
- Strengths and Weaknesses Matrix
- Situation Analysis
- Problems and Opportunities

Establish Measurable Goals and Objectives

Now you are ready to set goals and objectives. Most planners take the following steps:

- Define an overall goal or goals.
- Develop objectives for each group of identified problems and opportunities.
- Implement appropriate strategies for each objective.

But sometimes there is no time to follow all the steps formally. When pressed for time, develop one or two overall goals that apply to the total organization—the end results to achieve. Objectives, which are defined as the targets or results needed to be achieved in order to solve the problems, take advantage of the opportunities and reach the goal(s), may be fairly obvious and are sometimes stated or implied in the problem and opportunity statements themselves. Remember that goals and objectives should be measurable. A good overall business goal example is "to increase market share by X percent over the next three years," or "to increase net profit or return on investment by X percent within three years." A nonprofit organization's overall goal might be "to reduce dependency on federal and state dollars by X percent in three years."

In these examples, the goals are long-term (three years). Short-term goals can also be set when circumstances require that something be done within a year, six months, or sooner.

The following objectives statements are based on the problems and opportunities listed earlier for the two sample marketing plans. These statements list what a business or nonprofit organization might consider the important issues to address in their strategic business plans.

Statement of Objectives (Business)

1. To have an up-to-date and efficient production and distribution system within two years.
2. To achieve X percent of the 55-year-and-older market segment's business in three years.
3. To develop a unique image for the organization within a specific time frame.
4. To offer the best customer service in the industry by increasing the customer service from a level 5 to a level of 8 on a satisfaction scale within three years.
5. To reduce employee turnover to a level below the industry average within three years.

Statement of Objectives (Nonprofit)

1. To build sufficient funds to achieve the organization's mission.
2. To meet 100 percent of the community's teenage mental health needs within three years.
3. To acquire sufficient community contributions to make up the difference between total financial needs and federal funding.

Once the planning group agrees on the goals and objectives, write them on a flipchart, label them, and tape them on the wall.

Backing Into a Goal

What happens if you did not come up with any specific, measurable goals? It is difficult to develop meaningful strategies when no specific goals are defined. On the other hand, as long as there is a general goal, and the objectives are relative to the problems and opportunities previously defined, a group can and should move into the development of strategies, and then go "back into" setting specific goals.

Several group planning sessions I have lead had the general goal to increase market share or sales volume, but the group did not feel comfortable with a specific goal until it thought about what the organization could do. If the group set a goal—say, a 10-percent increase—members could be content with strategies that achieve that goal. But by leaving the goal undefined—at least temporarily—they came up with strategies that had the potential of producing a 25-percent increase.

This example illustrates the need to be flexible and creative in the group planning process. As long as the documented plan accurately depicts the organization at the present time, identifies the major problems and opportunities, sets some targets, recommends how to achieve the targets, and assigns responsibility for implementation, you have a plan—regardless of the labels and terms used to describe its parts. So do not let semantics and labels worry you. Keep the process moving. One person's goal may be another person's objective; one person's objective may be another person's strategy. The ultimate aim is that everyone in the planning group and in the organization agrees on the meaning and function of the planning terms and format.

Summary of Key Points

1. Define a realistic number of long-term or short-term goals to achieve within a specific time frame.

2. Develop a list of measurable objectives related to the problems and opportunities that help meet the goals.

3. Do not get bogged down with terminology or sequencing if a particular group working structure does not produce results. Be creative and maintain flexibility to work around productivity roadblocks.

4. Schedule a meeting to define the plan's implementation strategies.

5. Distribute copies of the agreed-upon goals, objectives, and any developed action plan before the next meeting.

CHAPTER 9
Meeting 4: Strategy Development

Up to this point, the group planning exercises have been primarily factual and analytical. The goals and objectives established in the last meeting stated **what** must be achieved, based on a thorough assessment of the current situation. Now it is time to be creative—that is, create ideas that will make things happen. The strategies developed in this meeting should describe **how** the group will achieve its overall goals and objectives.

Develop strategies by referring to the group's list of problems and opportunities. If this list was not produced because of time constraints, use the situation analysis as the key reference point.

Strategies could include developing a new product for a particular market segment, expanding into a new territory, or establishing a new pricing structure or advertising campaign. Sometimes strategies also include conducting research or restructuring current facilities. To develop strategies for a business or nonprofit organization, remember the four marketing Ps—product, price, place, and promotion (plus other categories, if you go that route). Develop strategies within these categories that address the problems, opportunities, and objectives defined in the previous planning exercises.

Refer to the sample situation analysis and problems and opportunities described for the business featured in chapter 7. The strategies developed for this type of scenario could include the following.

Strategies (Business)

1. Establish a task force to study production and distribution processes. Compare them with the most up-to-date and efficient systems available, and recommend appropriate changes.
2. Alter the product line and pricing structure to meet the unmet needs of the 55-year-and-older market segment.
3. Organize an advertising campaign that establishes a unique position for the company by emphasizing its product line and competitive pricing.
4. Develop an employee training and motivation or reward program to improve customer service levels.
5. Conduct research to determine the causes of employee turnover, and develop a plan based on the findings.

Strategies for the nonprofit organization featured in chapter 7 could include the following.

Strategies (Nonprofit)

1. Establish a task force to conduct an in-depth study of the needs associated with teenage mental illness in the community.
2. Develop services to meet the needs identified in 1.
3. Develop a public relations campaign to build community awareness of the services—especially the awareness of teenagers, parents, teachers, principals, doctors, and the business community.
4. Organize a major fund-raising campaign to build financial support (both public and private funds).

Creative-Thinking Exercises

Some interesting exercises that can be used to stimulate creativity are in the book, *Lateral Thinking* by Edward de Bono.[3] One exercise I have used based on my reading of this book involves taking a subject totally unrelated to the one in your plan and comparing it to the plan's subject. Ask the group to identify the new subject's characteristics and write them down the left side of a flipchart. Then ask the group to look at the characteristics in terms of what they might suggest about the subject of your plan. List these ideas down the right side of the flipchart. Here's an example of how to conduct this exercise.

A planning group was trying to develop new product strategies, but the members were having a difficult time getting their creative juices flowing. I suggested that we use this juxtaposition exercise. The group decided to focus on bananas for the exercise, and the following characteristics were noted:

---

[3] *Lateral Thinking*, Edward de Bono, Harper & Row.

■ Bananas grow in bunches.
■ They are bright yellow in color.
■ They are sold in grocery stores.

These characteristics, when compared to the product the group was addressing, translated into the following.

Bananas	**Products**
1. Bananas grow in bunches.	1. Develop a special package (bunch) for families.
2. They are bright yellow in color.	2. Add more color to the product.
3. They are sold in grocery stores.	3. Sell the product through area grocery stores.

Another creativity exercise I have used is called the "non" word exercise. Take a product, service, or even your organization, and list all of this subject's characteristics or process steps on a flipchart. Then put the prefix "non" in front of each feature or step, and ask the planning group to think about what changes this reversed meaning might suggest. This process can often produce radical new features or processes.

Remember that in all creativity exercises, there is no such thing as a dumb idea. Work to make the planning group members feel comfortable and open up their minds to outlandish ideas. Dare to be unique! If you are not, your organization or product will not be either.

To get customers to switch to your product or support your organization, you need to have a unique selling proposition—a reason why they should consider your product or service over competitors'. But building the unique features of a product, service, or event should be done during basic strategic business planning or marketing planning, not when you develop an advertising plan.

If a strategy has to do with improving the quality of a product or service, consider employing a group activity that is used in Japanese quality circles.[4] Draw a straight horizontal line across the middle of a flipchart, and draw a box at the end of the line on the right-hand side of the flipchart sheet. Then write a brief description of the problem or symptoms of the problem noted in the box. Then draw boxes along the horizontal line starting from the left-hand side of the page for each step in the product or service production and delivery process that leads to the problem. Label each box after the step it represents.

---

[4]*Lateral Thinking,* Edward de Bono, Harper & Row.

Figure 7: Continuous Improvement Exercise

Step 1	Step 2	Step 3	Step 4	Step 5	Step 6	Step 7	Problem or Symptom of Problem
a) Machinery or Process	a) ____	a ____)	a) ____	a) ____	a) ____	a) ____	
b) Manpower Performance	b) ____	b) ____	b) ____	b) ____	b) ____	b) ____	
c) Materials	c) ____	c) ____	c) ____	c) ____	c) ____	c) ____	
d) Methods	d) ____	d) ____	d) ____	d) ____	d) ____	d) ____	

Recommendations ____ ____ ____ ____ ____ ____
____ ____ ____ ____ ____ ____

The group then looks at each step and considers the following areas to determine where changes could be made to help solve the problem identified in the box on the right:

■ Machinery or process
■ Manpower performance
■ Materials
■ Methods

Write down recommended changes under the various boxes and consider them as possible strategies.

Often the planning group ends up with more strategies for a particular problem or opportunity than needed. If this happens, have the group choose which ones to implement—especially if the strategies conflict with each other.

Another simple group exercise is widely used to compare strategies. First, have the group decide on some appropriate criteria for choosing the product, such as profitability, feasibility, compatibility with other products, competitiveness, or originality. After the criteria are selected, assign a numerical value to each based on its relative importance. (The total for the criteria must add up to 100.) Score each proposed strategy against the criteria, using a scale from one to five, with five being the best. Multiply each criteria score by the weighting for the criteria. The following example shows a possible outcome. (There are many variations of this exercise that are also effective.)

Strategy A

Criteria	Score	Weighting		Final Score
Profitability	3	30	=	90
Feasibility	4	20	=	80
Compatibility	5	15	=	75
Competitiveness	2	20	=	40
Originality	2	15	=	30
		100		315

Strategy B

Criteria	Score	Weighting		Final Score
Profitability	4	30	=	120
Feasibility	4	20	=	80
Compatibility	5	15	=	75
Competitiveness	2	20	=	40
Originality	1	15	=	15
		100		330

As you can see, strategy B has a higher final score, so it may be the strategy to try or at least consider seriously. To score, get the group to reach a consensus on each score, or have them fill out individual score sheets and take the average of their scores. If you opt for the latter, it is best to do it twice. The first time, ask each member to read his or her scores aloud and explain the reasons for each score. Then ask the group to score again. On the second round, some may change their original scores, based on the group discussion.

After all the strategies are developed, allow some time for the group to review the objectives and strategies. Identify with a star or other mark those which are the most critical to the achievement of your goals. Prioritize the marked items in case the group is unable to do everything it would like. The objectives and strategies which are absolutely critical to your success must be the ones the group manages the closest.

The techniques described in this book helped the bank I worked with to become one of the most innovative financial institutions in New England. The organization's leaders believed in having a unique sales proposition, and most of its successful ideas came out of group planning sessions.

Revisit Initial Group Concerns

Before moving on to the next step, you have one more responsibility. Remember the list of Group Thoughts developed at the start of the planning process? The list should still be taped to the back wall. Be sure to revisit the Group Thoughts list to double check that everyone's thoughts, ideas, and concerns have been adequately addressed during the group planning process. After attending to this, the group can now develop an action plan—the most important step in the planning process.

Summary of Key Points

1. Develop strategies that relate directly to the problems and opportunities discovered during the situation analysis.

2. Use creativity exercises to stimulate group thinking when developing strategies.

3. Employ a group comparison exercise to determine which strategies should be implemented.

4. Prioritize the objectives and strategies that are most critical to helping the group achieve its goals.

5. Revisit the Group Thoughts list to make sure all concerns have been addressed.

6. Schedule a meeting to develop an action plan.

CHAPTER 10
Meeting 5: Action Plan Outlined

Without an action plan, you do not have a plan—only a study. Unfortunately, many so-called plans stop at the strategies step without addressing in detail what needs to be done by whom and by when in order to put the strategies into motion. An action plan addresses this step in the process. Without it nothing can happen.

The action plan is also important to the group planning process because this step can solidify the feelings of group ownership to the plan. If the group includes those who have the major responsibilities for the plan's execution, then they will know exactly what needs to be done and can commit themselves and their departments to the agreed-upon deadlines.

Tactics To Implement Strategies

An action plan deals with tactics. Sometimes, it is appropriate to develop strategies and tactics together on the same flipchart and label the complete set as the strategic action plan. One major advantage to this method is creating a discipline that forces the group to deal with each strategy adequately as it is developed.

Sometimes, on the other hand, it makes more sense to treat strategies and tactics separately because one action or tactic might cover two or more strategies. The way to proceed should be left up to the group members. But remember that every step in an action plan should be written on the flipchart along with the name of the person or department responsible for completing the steps by the specific deadlines.

If you decide to develop a separate action plan, the format is straightforward. Write each action or tactic needed to implement the plan on a flipchart. If two or more people are responsible for an action or tactic, make sure the planning group identifies one person as the team leader and underline that name. If you put a group in charge of something and do not appoint a leader, nothing will happen.

If you do decide to develop strategies and tactics together, the following approach is what it might look like.

Figure 3: Business Action Plan (Strategy 2)

Strategy	Tactics/Actions	Responsibilities	Deadlines
#2: Change product line to meet the needs of the 55 and over market at competitive prices.	Research the 55 and over market further to prioritize unmet needs and test for price sensitivity.	J. Jones and Research Dept.	1/15/94
	Conduct group planning sessions to develop a product plan.	P. Adams, J. Smith, L. Williams, P. Brook	2/15/94
	Present a product plan and financial breakdown to senior management.	P. Adams	3/1/94
	If accepted, establish new group to implement plan.	L. Davis, President	4/1/94

From this example, which addresses business strategy 2 in the example from chapter 9, the first tactic calls for research and the second calls for planning. This is an example of planning to plan. In this piece from an overall strategic plan, the planning group sees the need to develop a new line of products for people 55-years-old and older. However, based on the information the group members have, they cannot recommend that their company start manufacturing and selling such a line of products immediately. They know that they need more information, and a plan must be developed for the new line. As previously stated, it is okay to plan to plan.

The action plans for nonprofit organizations would develop the same way. The following figure is a typical series of actions or tactics for the nonprofit organization's strategies from chapter 9.

Figure 4: Strategic Action Plan (Nonprofit)

Strategy	Tactics/Actions	Responsibilities	Deadlines
Organize a major fund-raising campaign to provide financial support.	Appoint a fund-raising committee.	President of the organization	1/15/94
	Develop a list of individual and corporate prospects, as well as government grants.	Fund-raising committee and its chair	2/15/94
	Organize a group planning session to develop fund-raising plan.	Chair of fund-raising committee	3/1/94

At this point you may be asking, "These actions are so obvious, why write them down and assign deadlines?" Many planners and planning groups skip these steps, and ultimately that is why they fail. Unless people are "on the hook" to accomplish specific steps by certain dates, the plan has a good chance of fading away like a puff of smoke.

If the group decides to use a format similar to the ones illustrated above, you may want to develop all your tactics for each strategy before addressing who is responsible and setting deadlines. This approach keeps everyone's attention on what needs to be done, before worrying about who is going to do it. Otherwise, you risk getting sidetracked with personnel workload discussions that can interrupt the thought process. Treat these types of issues separately, but be sure to devote adequate time to them as well.

While leading a group through the action plan phase, you may notice a willingness—or eagerness—from some group members to offer their services to lead or participate in the various activities. This willingness indicates a sense of teamwork and enthusiasm that obviously developed during the group planning project. If one or two activities are not assigned by the end of this meeting, do not worry. The activities can be assigned after the meeting in consultation with the appropriate people.

One portion of the business action plan mentioned earlier calls for the development of another plan—a product plan. This new plan should take the same format as the overall strategic business plan. In this case, after further research into the 55-and-older market, the product planning group would participate in a series of group planning sessions similar to the ones for the organization as a whole. The group, with a facilitator's help, should analyze the collected research and develop a situation analysis based on the research findings, as well as the other relevant information on product, price, place/distribution, and promotion.

Then the group should identify the major problems and opportunities, and establish goals and objectives for the product's development. Develop strategies and an action plan that define the product's features and benefits, distribution, and pricing structure. After completing the product plan, another group should develop an advertising and promotion plan for the product, using the format described in chapter 14. The information so far explains that planning is an ongoing process, where one plan leads to another with each plan getting more specific and detailed.

A marketing plan format, with some minor changes, can also work for group planning of nonmarketing functions such as operations or training. Sometimes shortcuts can be taken during the process by starting with the development of appropriate objectives for the planning area, and then moving into the development of strategies, tactics, responsibilities, and time tables.

Looking at the wall and summarizing what was accomplished thus far in the strategic business planning process, the flipcharts should include the following:

- Group Thoughts
- Mission Statement of the Organization
- Purpose of the Planning Group
- Purposes of the Meetings
- Research Matrix
- Strengths and Weaknesses Matrix
- Situation Analysis
- Problems and Opportunities
- Goals and Objectives
- Strategies
- Action Plan (separate or combined strategies/action plan)

For an example of what your wall might look like, see the following pages.

Figure 5: Flow Chart of Group Planning Process

Purposes of Planning
1. To develop a directional planning document that is action-oriented
2. To create a system of participatory management—a team effort

Purpose of Preplanning Meeting
Introductory: To decide on the format and select planning group members

Purpose of Meeting #1
1. To record group thoughts
2. To review/change/develop mission statement, planning purposes, and format or process
3. To decide what we need to know in order to plan

Group Thoughts
1. "It's about time we did some planning; it's long overdue."
2. "We must be sure that everyone feels free to speak his or her mind."
3. "I'm convinced that there is opportunity; I hope this planning exercise recognizes that."
4. "To date, direction has come strictly from the top down; I hope this exercise will change that."
5. "I don't think we are doing our best in terms of customer service; I hope this plan will address that."
6. "Frankly I'm skeptical about the group approach to planning, but I'm willing to go along with it and hope it works."

Mission Statement
(Purpose of the Organization)
1. To manufacture and distribute a quality line of recreational exercise equipment
2. To excel in customer service
3. To be open to growth and expansion
4. To offer a rewarding work environment to our employees
5. To provide shareholders with an above-average return on their investment
6. To always act as a responsible corporate citizen

Information Needs	Who Will Get	When
1. Market share for ourselves and competitors	Jane	Date
2. Trends in the market: new products, market needs	Jane, Bill & Jack	Date
3. Strengths & weaknesses (ourselves & competitors)	Jack	Date
4. Customer satisfaction	Jack	Date
5. Comparison of our pricing with competitors'	Bill	Date
6. Compare our channels of distribution with competitors'	Sylvia	Date
7. Study our advertising vs. competitors'; how effective are we? What are competitors spending?	Peter	Date
8. Analysis of our production methods	Mary	Date

continued

Figure 5: Flow Chart of Group Planning Process (continued)

Purpose of Meeting #2
1. To develop situation analysis
2. To identify problems & opportunities

Business Situation Analysis
1. Our market share has remained steady over the past three years; currently we are in third place with 10% of the market.
2. The market is growing and shows promise of continued growth over the next several years, especially among those who are 55 years old and older.
3. Our major competitors are organization "A," which is in first place in market share, and organization "Y," which is in second place. Their market share trends are also steady.
4. Research shows that the market sees little difference between the three organizations' products.
5. The prices of the products are virtually the same.
6. Our production and distribution processes are out-of-date and costly.
7. Our profit margin is relatively low, not allowing much room for price modifications.
8. Market research shows some consumer needs currently are not being met by any of the products; particularly true for people 55 years old and older.
9. Research also indicates a lack of advertising awareness for any of the major competitors.
10. Research shows that our customer service level is in fifth place and dropping.
11. The rate of employee turnover is higher than the industry average.

Business Problems and Opportunities
1. **Problem:** Our production and distribution processes are outdated and costly. **Opportunity:** Solving this problem would increase our profit margins and allow us to consider more competitive pricing.
2. **Opportunity:** Meeting the unmet market needs of the 55-plus market.
3. **Opportunity:** Establishing a unique image for our business and its products.
4. **Problem:** Our customer service levels are unacceptably low; there is an opportunity to improve them.
5. **Problem:** Employee turnover is unacceptably high. **Opportunity:** Reducing turnover will improve morale and customer service.

Purpose of Meeting #3
1. To set overall goal(s) for the organization
2. To set objectives relative to the problems and opportunities

Overall Business Goals
1. To increase our share of market by X% over the next three years.
2. To increase our net profit by X% in the next three years.

Business Objectives (relative to Problems and Opportunities)
1. To have an up-to-date and efficient production and distribution system within two years
2. To meet the needs of the 55-plus market and achieve X% of that market segment's business in three years
3. To have a unique image for our business.
4. To offer the best customer service within our industry; increase our level of customer service satisfaction from a level of "5" on the satisfaction scale to a level of "8" within three years
5. To reduce employee turnover to a level below the industry average within three years

Figure 5: Flow Chart of Group Planning Process (continued)

Purpose of Meeting #4
1. To develop strategies to accomplish objectives and overall goals
2. To develop tactics for each strategy
3. To assign people to each tactic
4. To set a deadline for each tactic

Business Strategies
1. Establish a task force to study our production and distribution processes. Compare them with the most up-to-date, efficient systems available, and recommend appropriate changes.
2. Change our product line to meet the unmet needs of the 55-plus market at competitive prices.
3. Organize an advertising campaign that establishes a unique position for our company by emphasizing our unique product line and pricing.
4. Develop an employee training and motivation/reward program to improve customer service levels.
5. Conduct research to determine the causes of employee turnover, and develop a plan based on the findings.

Business Action Plan for Strategy 2

Strategy	Tactics/Actions	Responsibilities	Deadlines
#2: Change product line to meet the needs of the 55 and over market at competitive prices.	Research the 55 and over market further to prioritize unmet needs and test for price sensitivity.	J. Jones and Research Dept.	1/15/94
	Conduct group planning sessions to develop a product plan.	P. Adams, J. Smith, L. Williams, P. Brook	2/15/94
	Present a product plan and financial breakdown to senior management.	P. Adams	3/1/94
	If accepted, establish new group to implement plan.	L. Davis, President	4/1/94

Follow-up and Accountability

You now have an action-oriented plan, but nothing is going to happen without a series of follow-up meetings on a weekly, monthly, quarterly, or annual basis. People with assignments from the plan should attend the meetings and report on their progress. If there have been any delays, note them and the reasons for the delays on the plan document. The delays may even be significant enough to warrant a revision of the action plan or, at least, cause for rescheduling some key deadlines.

If your organization is a business, I recommend incorporating completed planning project assignments into the performance measurements of the employees responsible for the plan's implementation. Assuming these employees are measured against personal goals, the timely completion of assignments from group planning sessions should be included in the goals. Whoever is in charge of planning should report on the completion of assignments to the human resources department and the appropriate department heads.

Systematic follow-up and accountability cannot be stressed enough. They strongly influence the difference between a project's success and failure. They are as important as the planning process itself.

Summary of Key Points

1. Develop an action plan that includes the following information:
- step-by-step tactics for implementing each strategy
- names of persons and departments responsible for each tactic
- specific deadlines for completion of each step.

2. Type and distribute the action plan to all group members and others responsible for project implementation.

3. Hold periodic meetings (on an as-needed basis) to monitor the project's progress. Remedy problems and adjust scheduling when necessary.

4. Incorporate planning project responsibilities into employees' performance goals, and monitor employees' success in completing project assignments.

SECTION 3: A WORD ABOUT...

This section address three underlying components of organizational planning that strongly influence the effectiveness of plan implementation: visioning, financial analysis, and training.

Chapter 11   Visioning and Financial Analysis

Chapter 12   A Word to Trainers

CHAPTER 11
Visioning and Financial Analysis

As the term implies, **visioning** is a method of planning that develops an idea of how you would like your organization to look in the future. As said about planning in general, it is hard to imagine a group functioning without some vision of how it sees itself in the future. But many organizations fail because they do not have any vision of their future.

When Visioning Is Appropriate

The previous chapters described detailed formats for developing strategic business plans or marketing plans using the group approach to planning. To participate in this type of planning process, you should feel reasonably comfortable with your organization's internal environment and future direction. But what if you have some doubts about the organization's environment or its ability to live up to its stated purpose? Or what if your organization or group does not have any vision of itself in the future?

Situations such as these can provide a perfect opportunity to create a new or revitalized picture of an organization's future through a visioning process which can be conducted in a similar fashion to the group planning process described in previous chapters.

You may decide that you need to step back and develop a plan that is slightly different from the type of strategic plan described in this book. You may need a plan that is a little "softer," less "nuts and bolts"—one that does not accept the current organizational environment. Or you may want to do some visioning before you do strategic planning, incorporating the highlights of the visioning exercise in the strategic business plan.

Steps in the Visioning Process

As the process is described, you will notice similarities to the strategic business planning process. The most important thing to remember is to make the format fit the circumstances.

The first step, as in strategic planning, is to discuss and write down the group's thoughts. Second, write down the organization's purpose or mission as you see it right now. I recommend revisiting the statement of purpose after you have completed the visioning exercise to make any appropriate changes.

Third, have the group develop a list of organizational values. What qualities are considered most important to the organization? Do they include service to customers, dedication to quality, honesty, compassion, and self-motivation? What values do the group members feel are important to your organization's continued well-being? Write them on a flipchart and tape the sheets to the wall. Review this list after developing the organization's vision and strategies to make sure that they reflect the values the group considers most important.

Next, develop two lists: one for those things group members consider right about the organization and one for those things groups members consider wrong. For example, your organization makes a good product but offers poor service on repairs. Or a nonprofit organization might have a professional and dedicated staff but lacks support from its board of directors. To help develop such a list, refer the group to the four Ps—product, price, place or distribution, and promotion—as well as these categories: machinery (process), manpower (performance, caliber, and morale), materials, and methods. Developing such checklists can help stimulate thinking. However, the group will probably have no difficulty in coming up with lists of rights and wrongs.

After developing the checklists, examine what the future would be like if no changes were made within the organization—a kind of worst-case scenario. The fifth step in the visioning process is recording the group's answers to this question.

The group should now decide on its vision for the future. How would your group like the organization to look in three to five, or even 10 years? What should it look like? What should it be doing?

Strategic Action Plans

After answering the questions, the group should clearly see the gaps between what the organization will look like if changes are not made and what it will look like if the vision comes true. Identify those things that are pushing your organization towards the worst-case scenario and/or preventing it from achieving the vision. These things represent the major organizational issues for which the planning group needs to develop objectives, strategies, and action plans (as described in chapters 8, 9, and 10). Remember: Without an action plan you only have a study, and little or nothing will change.

You might find that one strategy calls for developing an ongoing strategic business planning process. That is fine! This is planning to plan, and you now know how to do it.

One final word: Compare the group's vision and strategies against its values list to ensure compatibility. And finally, revisit the purpose or mission statement to see if it needs changes after the group's visioning exercise.

Financial Analysis

Number crunching is a distinct part of every planning phase, and the process should never be undervalued or overlooked. Financial data are naturally part of the information and research gathered by a planning group. And if used correctly, numbers can help groups develop more thorough situation analyses. Numbers are also embedded throughout problem and opportunity areas, and financial feasibility strongly influences a group's goal and objective setting process. Finally, the availability of financial resources directly affects the whos, hows, whats, and whens that need to be specified in a strategic action plan. These facts make it imperative to include financial experts in any planning group.

Most likely, various numerical analyses and charts will be attached to a plan as appendices, including a pro forma income statement based on the strategies and tactics developed for the action plan. The planning group may also need to develop alternative strategies and tactics with corresponding financial analyses in order to maximize profits or get an overall plan accepted by senior management.

Ideas First, Numbers a Close Second

Your plan has to make financial sense, but ideas must always come first. If numbers are the planning group's first concern, budgeting drives planning, which extremely limits creativity and often makes the planning process futile. Instead, let planning drive the numbers. In most business situations, it is impossible to separate the numbers and the ideas entirely—they do and always will go together. But business is about meeting customers' needs and expectations, and people do not buy numbers. They buy products and services that are the direct results of creative thinking.

Even if you are good with numbers and have financial experts within the group, you may still need some guidance on using financial data to plan and make decisions. I recommend that the group use one of several reference guides, such as the *Vest Pocket M.B.A.* (Prentice-Hall), to help the group understand its budgeting and financial information.

Summary of Key Points

1. Visioning is the process used to define what an organization's position should be in the future.

2. To conduct a visioning exercise, group members should do the following:
• Discuss and record group thoughts.
• Define the organization's mission.
• List current organizational values.
• List the organization's good and bad or strong and weak points.
• Show what the organization's future would be like if no changes occur—a worst case scenario.
• Compare the "worst-case" scenario with the organization's wished-for vision.

• Define the issues that the planning group must address; those things that are driving the organization toward the worst-case scenario and/or preventing it from achieving the vision.

3. Develop a strategic action plan for those issues.

4. Group planning processes should include financial experts.

5. Strategic business plans must be thoroughly documented and financially feasible to get senior management support.

6. Ideas, not numbers, should drive any planning process.

CHAPTER 12
A Word to Trainers

Practice makes perfect. The most effective way for people to learn the group planning process is to participate in an actual planning project that addresses a real issue in their organization. Trainers who teach the group planning process and facilitation skills will find valuable information in this book to help them lead the group through an actual *Write on the Wall* planning exercise.

Here are some suggestions for ways to enhance a group planning and facilitation workshop.

Preplanning
1. Require trainees to read *Write on the Wall* prior to the workshop.
2. Use a real-life situation in your organization or obtain an appropriate case history, and distribute it to the trainees as additional reading before the workshop.
3. Select an appropriate setting for conducting the workshop.
4. Obtain all materials needed to conduct the workshop.
5. Learn as much about each trainee as possible.

During the Workshop
1. Present an overview of the planning process and the real-life situation or case history, and answer any questions the group may have about either one.
2. Practice what you preach. Define the purpose of the workshop with the group, and initiate a Group Thoughts exercise.
3. When appropriate, select individuals to lead parts of the meetings.
4. Break into smaller groups.

5. Ask each of the smaller groups to develop a plan based on the real-life situation or case history. Alternate the role of the facilitator in each of the groups so all trainees get an opportunity to lead a group through a portion of the planning process.

6. As the trainer, circulate among the groups as they develop their plans to give them appropriate guidance. Remember to concentrate on individuals' performances as facilitators and the quality of the groups' overall plans rather than the feasibility of specific implementation strategies they develop. Did the trainees encourage individual participation, keep their groups focused, and keep the process moving? Did each trainee capsulize the situation and identify the problems and opportunities? Do they understand the differences between goals, objectives, strategies, and tactics?

7. Point out good examples of each part of the planning process as they occur during the group exercises, such as successfully identifying problems and opportunities or defining concrete goals, objectives, and strategies.

8. Trainers also have to decide how to review individual performance with each trainee. Remember the Group Thoughts. Be sure to review the thoughts with the whole group before ending the workshop. In your final reviews, make certain that you address all the trainees' expectations and concerns.

Workshop Follow-up

Each trainee should be given the opportunity to lead a group in developing a complete plan. Ideally, the trainer should observe the trainee's first group planning meeting and critique the performance with the fledgling facilitator, following the completion of the meeting. From then on, it is a matter of improving with experience.

Summary of Key Points

1. The best way to teach group planning and facilitation skills is to conduct a mock group planning exercise or workshop.

2. A trainer's workshop pre-planning should include the following:
• Distribute all reading and reference materials prior to the scheduled date of the workshop.
• Select an appropriate setting for the workshop.
• Obtain all materials needed to conduct the workshop.
• Learn about individual trainee backgrounds.

3. During a workshop, a trainer should do the following:

• Provide an overview of the planning process and workshop contents.
• Serve as an example of a good facilitator.
• Ensure that there is both individual and group participation during each planning phase.
• Provide assistance to the trainees throughout their planning exercises, and recognize success.
• Decide how to conduct trainee reviews.

4. Following a workshop, the trainer should evaluate each new facilitator's real-life performance in a group planning situation.

SECTION 4: PLAN VARIATIONS

These closing chapters present specific variations for the group planning processes.

CHAPTER 13
Advertising Planning

Planning for advertising is easier if you have a basic strategic business plan such as the one described in the last several chapters. This plan forces the kind of homework that helps the group develop any advertising planning. You identify a product or service, which is based on identified needs and wants of the market. You define a target or goal for meeting the needs, and you address pricing and distribution issues. After all, advertising does not exist in a vacuum. It is part of a synergy, and that is what you have when you have a marketing or strategic business plan.

However, the real world of planning is not always perfect, so you may have to "punt." If you do not have a marketing or strategic business plan, develop some "background" information on which to base your advertising plan. Include as much background information as possible from such areas as the performance history of the product, service, or organization; market share data; competitor information; advertising to date and its success; pricing history; current pricing; and distribution and sales information. This information can serve the same function as the situation analysis in strategic business planning—to determine where you are before planning where to go.

As I advocate the group approach to advertising planning, the background information should be given to your group before the first planning meeting. If this is impossible, then distribute the material at the beginning of the meeting and review it. Or if you do not have a list of needed "background" information by meeting time, develop one with the group at the meeting and write it on a flipchart.

How a Group Can Plan Advertising

How can a group of people be involved in developing something as creative as advertising? First of all, I am talking about planning for advertising, not creating it. Much advertising is ineffective because it is not properly planned. Much time also can be wasted in developing advertising that is unplanned because advertising agencies are often not properly briefed by their clients. So when the agency representatives come back with their "great ideas," they discover that the client had something entirely different in mind. They may even find that their entire proposal is based on an incorrect premise.

An organization might use an advertising agency, freelance writer, artist, local newspaper, radio, or TV station to create its advertising, but it still has the responsibility to properly brief these creators before they develop an advertising campaign.

The best way to plan for advertising and be certain that the creators are properly informed is by using the group approach. This approach works for the same reasons as those for strategic planning: You get the benefits of group dynamics, develop consensus among the major players, enhance communication, develop enthusiasm, and create a team spirit from the beginning.

Group Participants

The group to develop an organization's advertising planning may be different than the group that worked on the marketing or strategic business plan. Usually during the strategic business planning process, advertising-related strategies and tactics are assigned to a specific subgroup that may not include members of the strategic planning group.

In a business organization, the advertising planning group may consist of the marketing manager, advertising manager, product manager, sales manager, advertising agency account executive, and often the copywriter from the agency. In a nonprofit organization, the group responsible for advertising planning may be the same group that put together the directional plan, or it could be the publicity committee. In either case, the group assembled for advertising planning should have a stake in the advertising. So in addition to the advertising creators, the group should also include those responsible for approving the final advertising program and materials.

Working With Agencies

An organization that chooses to work through an advertising agency should consider the agency a part of the organization and work closely with its representatives. Take the agency's people into your confidence and make them part of the team. Unfortunately, many organizations treat their agency people like outsiders and poorly communicate what they want even after strategic decisions are made. This often leads to ineffective advertising campaigns and promotions.

Plan Format

Many basic group planning rules covered in the previous chapters apply here as well, so this section concentrates on the format for your flipchart planning sessions. Again, assume that the organization has either a marketing or strategic business plan as a base, or that ample background information has been collected and analyzed.

1. Budgeting. At the risk of sounding contradictory, the bottom-line budget figure should be the first thing considered and noted on a flipchart during the first advertising planning session. For practical purposes, you need to develop an ad campaign within a specific budget target. When the budget is not considered up front, much time is wasted planning advertising campaigns that cannot be funded.

Be sure to show if a program developed within the current budget is inadequate. In such cases, a new budget may need to be considered in order to produce the most effective advertising scheme.

2. Marketing Goals and Objectives. Restate the goals and objectives developed for the organization's marketing or strategic business plan. These goals and objectives are targets for the whole organization, and advertising has a role to play in achieving them. But the role, varies depending on the nature of the business. Therefore, specific advertising objectives complementing the organization's overall planning efforts should be developed.

3. Advertising Objectives. Describe the role of advertising plays for the organization. Is it meant to produce sales? Or is it meant to support the sales efforts of a salesforce? Looking at a sales spectrum, where would advertising fall in the list of priorities? Does it have 100 percent responsibility to produce your organization's sales? Or does it have 10 percent or somewhere in the middle? The answer to these questions will determine the kind of advertising you need. One hundred percent responsibility for sales might call for coupon or catalog advertising. Regular media advertising might be needed to support a network of sales outlets. Maybe the purpose of the advertising is to drive customers into a particular store or event. The planning group should decide on the objectives for each advertising campaign and relay this information to the ad agency.

When developing advertising, remember that it represents only one piece of the total picture. Advertising alone cannot do everything. The organization must supply the right products at the right price to the right market using a well-trained and motivated staff. So while it is important to recognize the importance of advertising, you must also give it a realistic objective.

4. Product (Features/Benefits). Next in the advertising planning process, list on a flipchart the features of the product, service, or event, as well as its benefits, such as what it does for the customer, the basic needs it meets, money savings, and consumers' health or wealth factors. Remember that while features may be important, benefits are what people want and buy. So that is what advertising should emphasize. What does the group think the benefits are? Put all these answers on the flipchart.

5. Market Segmentation. Refer to the marketing or strategic business plan to find the description of the market for the product, service, or event being advertised. Who are the customers? What are they like? Where do they live? How many are there? List all this information on the flipchart. The people who create the actual advertising materials and recommend media usages will need all this information.

6. Messages. Ask the group the following questions. What is likely to motivate the customer to buy the product, service, or event? What is the most compelling message to communicate to the market, based on motivation plus the information revealed in the marketing or strategic business plan? Do not try to write the advertising copy here. Simply work together with the agency's people to create a copy platform on which to base the actual advertising copy or messages. Revisit the product benefits information and market description. Ask the group for key words and phrases. Jot them down, and try to weave them into a coherent message. Write this message on the flipchart.

7. *Media.* What are the most likely media to use to reach your market effectively and efficiently with the message you want to communicate? I use the word "likely" because you probably should not make your final media choices at this group planning session. Instead discuss media preferences from a preliminary standpoint, and get people's thoughts and ideas on the table. If you employ an advertising agency, you would want its representatives to provide media recommendations based on their expert analysis of the situation. If you do not have an agency, then someone in the organization needs to check with the advertising sales representatives of various local media (newspapers, radio, TV, and direct mail companies) to do some comparison shopping. Your budget is going to influence strongly your media choices. However, look at such items as overall advertising objectives, relative cost of reaching 1,000 people, media appropriateness for the message, and the organization's advertising history. If, for example, the message depends heavily on visual support, you may not find radio effective.

8. *Promotion/Merchandising.* At this point, the group needs to think about such issues as sales contests, trade shows, coupons, point-of-sale materials such as posters and brochure racks, video displays, and folders, and grand opening events. Many organizations know from experience that you often cannot rely solely on advertising to do the whole job. For maximum effectiveness, support advertising with other forms of promotion that usually complement each other—the advertising informs and stimulates the customer, the merchandising material reminds the customer to make a purchase at the point of sale, and the promotional material gives the needed push to make a positive decision.

9. *Budget Revisited.* Reevaluate the projected budget by asking these tough questions: Is the budget that was set at the beginning of the advertising planning session going to be enough to do what was just planned? If more money is needed, can it be justified? Will the program produce the results called for by the marketing or strategic business plan? Number crunchers can help come up with the appropriate financial

analysis. If changes are needed, the group must state the case for budget revision clearly and concisely.

10. Outcome Measurements. Next, the group must decide how the organization will measure the success or failure of its advertising. If advertising does not bear the full burden of the sales results, do not measure its return on investment (ROI) solely on sales volumes. While sales may be a factor in the ROI analysis, market awareness levels of the organization's advertising efforts also should be measured. If the target market is aware of the organization's advertising but still does not buy the product, it might be due to the product or its price—not the effectiveness of the advertising. In such cases, use market research tactics to explore what the customer got from the advertising. For example, did the advertising accurately communicate its message? Ideally, this should also be researched before launching a campaign to make sure advertising is on the right track.

If, on the other hand, advertising carries all or almost all the burden for sales, or it is meant to produce inquiries in the form of coupons, telephone calls, or personal visits, you simply need to keep track. However, this is not going to happen by itself. The group must decide how to do it and state in the action plan who will be responsible for doing it or seeing that it gets done. This may involve forming another planning group to develop a tracking plan.

11. Action Plan. Developing the action plan is the final step. The planning group needs to review what it has recorded on the flipcharts, and develop an action plan that spells out who has to do what, by when. If the organization employs an advertising agency, the action plan should direct the agency to develop the following proposed creative items by a specific date:
- Print copy and layout
- TV story boards
- Radio scripts
- Brochures
- Proposed media selection and schedules
- Accompanying cost estimates

The agency's proposals should be based on the plan the group just developed. If the organization did not hire an ad agency, assign the above tasks to an internal committee or freelance advertising expert. Assign tasks not normally performed by an agency, such as developing sales contests, tracking sales, inquiries, or visits, to your own people. Let us review the steps you completed and taped to the wall to develop this advertising plan.

■ Formulate a budget.
■ Set market goals and objectives.
■ Set advertising objectives.
■ Define the product features/benefits
■ Identify the market segmentation.
■ Form the appropriate messages.
■ Explore media options.
■ Explore promotion/merchandising options.
■ Revisit the budget.
■ Choose measurement methods.
■ Develop an action plan.

After these issues are addressed, the people who will create the advertising and recommend media have the direction they need. The organization also has a clearer understanding of needed advertising and promotion.

Accountability

If a system of regular follow-up meetings is not set up to assess progress and note and reward completion of tasks, you may have just wasted a lot of time. Even nonprofit people and volunteer boards need to be held accountable for the timely completion of tasks assigned to them. To ensure the plan's success, the group must decide how often to assess progress, and set up a system for recognizing and rewarding those who meet their goals.

Summary of Key Points

1. Provide as much background information as possible to the group planners before the first planning meeting.

2. Thoroughly brief the planners on the purpose of the advertising scheme to develop.

3. Ensure that the group planners selected all have a stake in the advertising outcome.

4. Work closely with ad agency representatives.

5. Set realistic, measurable advertising objectives.

6. Decide how to assess the plan's progress, and set up a follow-up system for recognizing and rewarding those who meet goals.

CHAPTER 14
Public Relations Planning

The best definition of public relations (PR) I have come across goes something like this: "Public relations is doing good and telling people about it." I like this definition because it covers the two things that PR is most about: doing and telling—and it puts doing first.

Unfortunately, many organizations' and people's views vary widely on what public relations is about. Many believe that good PR can cover up something bad, but it does not work that way—at least not for long. Making a bad organization or situation look good using PR is like trying to make a poor product or service succeed through effective advertising. In marketing, good advertising often helps to ensure that a poor product or service fails sooner.

I believe the same holds true for public relations. In PR, you need something good to talk about. Much PR effort goes into the **doing** of something good—sometimes more effort than into the **telling.**

However PR, like advertising, does not exist in a vacuum. PR efforts also require direction from the organization's overall plan. PR should, like advertising, help to promote the organization and its products, services, or events. Therefore, you need to review the organization's overall strategic business plan to identify the groups or markets that are important to the organization's success. PR efforts need to address these groups, in addition to other groups such as shareholders, members, employees, government, and the community. In PR, these groups are often called **publics.**

Again, I advocate that PR planning, like strategic business and advertising planning, be developed using the *"Write On the Wall"* group planning approach. But this time, the group should consist of people in the organization who have the most at stake in each of the publics that matter the most to the organization's success. The PR planning group also should include a staff person or consultant responsible for implementing the actual PR programs and events.

PR Plan Format

After the group is selected, the group leader and a facilitator should run a meeting or series of meetings similar to the format discussed in previous chapters. During the meetings, the plan should be written out in bulleted form on flipchart sheets and taped to the wall.

The following format can help to guide you through the process. It is almost identical to the marketing plan format, except for the additional sections that relate to messages and budgeting. When using this format, the group lists the publics that are most important to the organization. Then it develops a plan that addresses the following questions for each of the publics.

1. Group/Public. What are the particular group's or public's needs?

2. Situation. What is our situation relative to this group or public?

3. Problems/Opportunities. What particular problems need to be addressed? What opportunities can be seized?

4. Objectives. What objectives should the organization establish in relation to this group? What is the organization trying to do relative to this particular public?

5. Messages. What basic messages should the organization communicate to this group?

6. Strategies. How will the objectives be achieved? What programs, events, or activities should be implemented? How will these be organized? What press releases or feature stories need to be developed?

7. Tactics. What steps must be taken to accomplish each strategy? Who is responsible for each by when?

8. Budget. How much will these efforts cost? How much money is available?

Here is how the above looks in chart form:

Public Relations Planning								
Groups/ Publics	Situation	Problems/ Opportunities	Objectives	Messages	Activities/ Events	Media	Budget	Actions

If this format is used, tape several blank flipchart sheets together on the wall. Draw the chart. The planning team should then fill in the squares, addressing one group or public at a time.

When considering activities or events, do not overlook the ones already associated with the organization. If current activities are not adequate to cover the identified important publics, consider creating new events. An activity or event can run the gamut from a seminar to luncheon to road race. Whatever the activity, it should be appreciated by the group the organization is trying to influence, and it should convey the kind of message and image the team wants to convey. The group planning approach can be a most effective way to plan and give your PR staff direction. It can also be effective in persuading senior management that more PR work needs to be done.

Coping With Bad Publicity

Unfortunately, PR is not always about organizing activities and events and issuing press releases to announce good things. PR is also about dealing with the press when unfortunate things happen. Group planning can be most helpful here as well. As soon as you find out that something has happened that will be of interest to the media, schedule a meeting with the people in the organization who know the facts and those who set policy. Conduct a *Write on the Wall* session with these people to develop a situation analysis, identify problems, decide on objectives, and then decide exactly what to say and do (i.e., strategies/tactics).

After establishing the strategies, the PR or publicity department can prepare a statement or press release, send copies to the appropriate people in the organization for review, and get ready for press calls. If the media call before such a meeting is held, tell them that the matter is being looked into and when a statement is developed, they will be called back. Always ask for their deadlines and try to meet them. If you know you cannot meet their deadline, be honest with them up front and let them know. And remember, just like any other type of plan, a PR action plan requires follow-up to check progress and sustain accountability.

Summary of Key Points

1. Begin public relations planning by identifying and listing the most important publics to the company.

2. Conduct a situation analysis, pointing out key problems and opportunities.

3. Decide what the organization should do for each group, and define the messages the company should communicate to each of its publics.

4. Identify actions that the organization can take to achieve its goals.

5. Develop a financial analysis, detailing the costs of the planning effort.

6. Develop a systematic approach to handling bad publicity.

AFTERWORD

You are now ready to start the *Write on the Wall* group planning process in your organization. As you get more experience in this process, you can alter the formats to suit your situation and style. You may also want to expand the process to penetrate deeper into your organization, developing your own formats to do that.

Group planning will really start to get interesting when you begin creating your own formats and find new uses for them. But to perfect your group planning and facilitation skills, you may want to study group psychology and communications. Read up on those subjects, and do not be afraid to experiment. It was fun sharing this information with you. Happy *Writing on the Wall!*

About the Author

Terence Goodwin has extensive experience in marketing, communications, public relations, and group planning, most of which was acquired while working in the financial services industry. He has shared his approach to group planning with numerous for-profit and nonprofit organizations. A native of Canada, Goodwin is a graduate of Fordham University in New York. He is currently a free-lance planning consultant, living in Portland, Maine.

Acknowledgement

I would like to extend my sincere appreciation to Janet F. Lavenger. Without her expert advice and editorial assistance, this manuscript may never have been published.

APPENDIX:
Sample Charts and Checklists

Strategic Planning Formats

Option A

1. Mission Statement
2. Informational Needs Assessment
3. Situation Analysis
4. Problems and Opportunities
5. Goals
6. Objectives
7. Strategies
8. Action Plan

Option B

1. Mission Statement
2. Informational Needs Assessment
3. Situation Analysis
4. Problems and Opportunities
5. Goals
6. Issue Areas
    a.) Problems and Opportunities
    b.) Objectives
    c.) Strategies
    d.) Action Plan

} For Each Issue Area

Research Matrix

	Questions	**Answers**				
		Have	Don't Have	Where to Get Answers	Who Will Get Answers	Deadlines
Products (Ours & Major Competitors)						
Price (Ours & Major Competitors)						
Place or Distribution (Ours & Major Competitors)						
Promotion (Ours & Major Competitors)						
Other						

Strengths and Weaknesses Matrix

	Product	Price	Place or Distribution	Production	Promotion
Competitor A					
Competitor B					

Code: + Better Than Competitors
              − Not As Good As Competitors
              0 No Difference Between Organization and Its Competitors

Creative-Thinking Exercises

Juxtaposition Exercise

Pick totally unrelated object.

Name of product or service being planned.

_____

_____

List characteristics of that object.

What do the characteristics listed on the left suggest about possible changes to product?

a) _____

a) _____

b) _____

b) _____

c) _____

c) _____

d) _____

d) _____

e) _____

e) _____

"Non" Word Exercise

List all the characteristics, features, steps of your product, service, or process.

Put the word "non" in front of each of the items on the left.

What changes do each of the "non" phrases suggest?

a) _____

a) Non _____

a) _____

b) _____

b) Non _____

b) _____

c) _____

c) Non _____

c) _____

d) _____

d) Non _____

d) _____

e) _____

e) Non _____

e) _____

Continuous Improvement Exercise

Step 1	Step 2	Step 3	Step 4	Step 5	Step 6	Step 7	Problem or Symptom of Problem
a) Machinery or Process	a) _____	a) _____	a) _____	a) _____	a) _____	a) _____	
b) Manpower Performance	b) _____	b) _____	b) _____	b) _____	b) _____	b) _____	
c) Materials	c) _____	c) _____	c) _____	c) _____	c) _____	c) _____	
d) Methods	d) _____	d) _____	d) _____	d) _____	d) _____	d) _____	

Recommendations _____ _____ _____ _____ _____ _____
_____ _____ _____ _____ _____ _____

Exercise for Comparing Alternative Strategies

(Repeat for each strategy and compare total final scores)

Criteria	Score (1 to 5, 5 is best)	Weighting (Total = 100)	Final Scores (Score × Weighting)
Profitability	_____	_____	_____
Feasibility	_____	× _____	= _____
Compatibility	_____	× _____	= _____
Competitiveness	_____	× _____	= _____
Originality	_____	× _____	= _____
	_____	× _____	= _____
		100 _____	**Total Final Score**

Advertising Planning Format

1. Advertising Budget
2. Marketing Goals and Objectives
3. Advertising Objectives
4. Product Features and Benefits
5. Description of Market
6. Motivations and Messages
7. Media
8. Promotion/Merchandising
9. Budget Revisited
10. Measurement
11. Action Plan

Public Relations Planning

Groups/ Publics	Situation	Problems/ Opportunities	Objectives	Messages	Activities/ Events	Media	Budget	Actions

Visioning Format

1. Mission Statement
2. Values
3. What's right with the organization?
4. What's wrong with the organization?
5. What will happen if no changes are made? (worst-case scenario)
6. What is our vision for the future? (way we'd like organization to be)
7. Major issues to be addressed—(things that are pushing the organization toward the worst-case scenario and preventing it from achieving its vision)
8. Objectives
9. Strategic Action Plan
   a) Strategies
   b) Tactics
   c) Responsibilities
   d) Timetables